The Author

Marion Field was brought up and educated [text obscured] teacher, she taught in Canada and Uganda, returning to [text obscured] position as Head of English in a comprehensive school. She took early retirement to concentrate on writing. She has had eleven books published, as well as a number of articles. As well as playing tennis regularly, she acts with a local drama group and is an active member of her local Anglican church.

WOKING:
THE WAY WE WERE

Marion Field

FORT PUBLISHING LTD

First published in 2005 by Fort Publishing Ltd, Old Belmont House,
12 Robsland Avenue, Ayr, KA7 2RW

© Marion Field, 2005

All rights reserved. No part of this publication may be reproduced, stored in a retrieval system, or transmitted, in any form or by any means, electronic, mechanical, photocopying, recording or otherwise, without the prior permission of the publishers and copyright holders.

Marion Field has asserted her right under the Copyright, Designs and Patents Act, 1988 to be identified as the author of this work.

Typeset by Senga Fairgrieve

Graphic design by Mark Blackadder

Photographs by author unless otherwise stated

Printed by Bell and Bain Ltd, Glasgow

ISBN 0-9547431-3-X

ACKNOWLEDGEMENTS

Mr John Bassett, Mrs Margaret Etheridge, Miss Sheila Gaff, Mrs Angela Jones, Mrs Peggy Methold, Mrs Lisa Stuart-Runsey, Mr Ken Turner, Mr Iain Wakeford, Surrey History Centre, Woking Borough Council, Woking Public Library, Woking Town Twinning Association, *Woking News and Mail*.

Marion Field, Woking, 2005

INTRODUCTION: WOKING BEFORE 1900

The name, 'Wochingas', later corrupted to 'Woking', first appeared in early Saxon records relating to the foundation of a minster dedicated to St Peter. Later it became a royal manor and was mentioned in the Domesday Book in 1086. Soon after ascending the throne, William I built St Peter's church on the site of the wooden Saxon church. This became the parish church of 'Woking' for centuries.

Over the next four hundred years Woking Manor had various 'owners' – not all of them royal – but in 1485 it came into the possession of Lady Margaret Beaufort, the grandmother of Henry VIII. She transformed the original manor house into a royal palace and lived in it for much of her life. It was surrounded by a moat and the entrance to it was by a drawbridge. When she died in 1509, she bequeathed the manor of Woking to her grandson so it once again became a royal possession.

Henry VIII liked Woking and used the palace as his summer residence. As the area was part of the royal forest of Windsor, the King could enjoy one of his favourite pastimes – hunting deer. Henry's successors were not as attracted to the place as he had been and in 1618 James I sold the manor of Woking to one of his favourites, Sir Edward Zouch. He demolished the palace and built himself a new manor house at Hoe Bridge Place with some of the materials. At his new abode, he entertained both James I and his son, Charles, but the strong royal connection with Woking was lost and never regained.

The surrounding park reverted to farmland and a number of new houses were built. Sir Edward renovated St Peter's church adding a gallery under the west door. He was also responsible for introducing pine trees to Woking. The town was already in decline and by the end of the seventeenth century Woking was a small agricultural town. There were no new developments until 1796 when the Basingstoke canal, running from Basingstoke to London, was completed and passed through Woking transporting coal, timber, groceries and earthenware.

However, when the railway was built in the middle of the nineteenth century, the boats could not compete with the speed of the trains and use of the canal dwindled. On 12 May 1838 the first steam train from Vauxhall trundled into Woking, where it terminated. Later the line was extended to Southampton. The railway put Woking firmly on the map.

A few years later it had another claim to fame. Land was needed for a burial ground outside London and 400 acres in Woking were sold to the Necropolis

Company. On 7 November 1854 the Bishop of Winchester consecrated the land for burial. Later, when cremation became legal, a crematorium was built in Woking and the first cremation took place in 1885.

During the latter part of the nineteenth century a local landowner, George Rastrick, bought much of the land on the south side of the station forcing 'new' Woking to develop on the north side. Woking owes its later growth to the railway and the crematorium.

1900

Floods

The floods that started off the new century were the worst in the area for over forty years. Old Woking resembled 'an inland sea' as torrents of water hurtled down from the Guildford hills cutting off the area from the rest of the town. In some houses the water was several feet deep. One unoccupied house that had fallen into decay had some unexpected visitors. A gaggle of geese took advantage of the water and amused themselves by swimming in one window and out of another.

As the roads were impassable, a boat was used to rescue a young horse that had been left in a field submerged in water up to its knees. Hay was floated on the water for it to eat but the horse refused to cooperate, causing the boat almost to capsize. Fortunately there were no casualties and, when the horse was finally rescued, it was none the worse for its experience.

A bridge in Guildford collapsed, and more water flowed down towards the village; as it swirled past the Guildford brewery, it swept up a number of beer barrels and Old Woking residents found they had acquired a floating public house! When the water finally subsided, mud and slime remained as a reminder of the worst floods for years.

Boer War

In January one hundred men from the second battalion, the East Surrey Regiment, left Inkerman Barracks in Knaphill early in the morning for service in the Boer War in South Africa. Reveille had sounded at half past two in the morning and at four thirty the regiment was on parade before leaving Brookwood station at five o'clock.

One of the men, Colour Sergeant Briffett, was later very lucky when he was shot in an engagement. The bullet struck his pocket knife, pierced a tin of food and went through a photograph before piercing his thigh. Another soldier from the same regiment was also wounded and wrote to his parents in Woking: 'You see most horrible sights during an engagement and you have a most horrible feeling.'

The son of Mrs Bloom of Fairlight, Maybury Road was in the Rifle Brigade and wrote to her about the relief of Ladysmith:

> I passed through the terrible battle to the relief of Ladysmith quite safely. The battle lasted fifteen days and we were fighting for thirteen and a half days. . . . We crossed the Tugela and were put in the firing line where we remained for

thirty-six hours and during that time we had four officers and seventy-five rank and file hit. Then we supported the naval guns and did not get into the firing line until General Buller's manoeuvres for the position were complete.... The Boers received such a severe drubbing ... that they fled in a great hurry and our cavalry reached Ladysmith at midnight on Tuesday.... Now the Boers are retiring and taking up a position at Dundee again. I pity them. I am very thankful we were able to relieve the beleaguered garrison as they were almost in their last extremities... I thank God from my heart that He has brought me through so far without a scratch.

Fire brigade farce

The fire brigade didn't have a very good year. Called to a fire at the laundry in Maybury Road, there was a prompt response. Unfortunately while their hose was trained on the laundry, a spark from the engine targeted their old handcart, which went up in flames. Hurriedly turning the engine to attack the new fire, they ran over the hose, cutting off the water supply. Handcart and laundry were left to burn.

Drunk in charge of a horse

On 29 March a Woking cab driver, Mr T. J. Drew, was stopped by a constable and arrested for being drunk while driving a horse-and-trap. At Guildford police court he pleaded guilty and was fined £1.

Engine derailed

The derailment of an engine at eleven o'clock on a hot day in July caused chaos to the railway timetable. The engine had been pulling some empty coaches towards Woking station but it missed the points, which had probably contracted because of the intense heat.

The rest of the trains were diverted to the local lines causing a great deal of delay and a group of workmen was hurriedly dispatched to the scene. They had a difficult job. The fifty-ton engine had just taken on 2,000 gallons of water and in the heat it was no easy task to move the vehicle and repair the damaged metal points. It took the men over four hours. The trains that were able to run took over an hour to travel from Weybridge to Woking. However, there was one train that was not delayed: the royal train carrying the Prince of Wales passed through Woking just after midday on its way to London.

Because of the derailment, some trains were halted at Byfleet causing the passengers much discomfort on this stifling July day. In an attempt to get fresh air, some daredevil souls, including one young lady, edged along the footboards of the trains clutching the door handles for safety. The guards and engine drivers, meanwhile, seized the opportunity to pick wild flowers in a nearby field. It was late in the evening when the train service returned to normal.

Gas wins

Although Woking had followed the trend of replacing gas light with electricity, it was not a success. The power station was situated in North Street and the power supply continually failed. Frustrated, the council refused to renew the power station's contract for electric lights in Woking's streets. Instead, they reverted to the gas company and Woking was once again lit by gas. It was also cheaper, a further bonus for ratepayers.

Bolting horse

In November, Woking pedestrians were scattered when a horse attached to a four-wheeled vehicle bolted up Church Street and Goldsworth Road. The horse and its attachment, owned by Mr E. J. Waters, a fly proprietor, had been standing outside the stables in Church Street when it got bored and decided to go for a run.

After several unsuccessful attempts by passers-by to catch it, a policeman grabbed hold of it and, after being dragged some distance, he finally managed to stop it on the brow of the hill near the nursery in Goldsworth Road. Had he not done so, there might have been a serious accident as a number of cyclists were heading up the hill from the opposite direction.

1901

Death of Queen Victoria

Queen Victoria died on 22 January and on Saturday, 2 February, the train carrying her coffin passed through Woking just after ten o'clock in the morning on its way from Portsmouth to London. A beautiful wreath had been on display at the station: it consisted of a crown of violet-and-white flowers and had been made by Messrs Jackman and Sons. It was presented by 250 rail workers and the inscription read: 'A tribute of affection from all grades of railway men at Woking station.'

Later that day the funeral took place at Windsor. At the same time a memorial service was held in Christ Church in the centre of Woking. Because of the importance of the occasion, the vicar had invited a number of nonconformist ministers to take part.

The church was packed with people from all walks of life and from different churches in the town. Also present were members of the district council. It was a solemn and memorable occasion that would long be remembered by those present.

Country bumpkin

Farmer Olife of Round Hill farm, Woking, decided to take a day off and travelled to London to see the sights. In the Strand he met two ladies with whom he struck up an acquaintance. They told him they were Miss Amelia Harris, a dressmaker, and Miss May Palmer, a pianist. He invited them to join him for a drink and, after a certain amount of persuasion, they accepted.

But they were not what they seemed. The farmer's watch mysteriously disappeared and the young ladies found themselves in the dock at Westminster police court. Perhaps Mr Olife should have stayed in Woking to look after his cows.

The headless corpse

Early one Wednesday morning in March a decapitated body was found on the London and South West railway line near the wooden bridge at St John's. It belonged to a 30-year-old man named Williams. He was a casual worker employed by Messrs Aird and Co. on the railway-extension works between Woking and Brookwood. Although he had worked for the company for three years, no one seemed to know anything about him and it was not known where he lived. He had last been seen alive at St John's on the previous Monday afternoon.

George Pucket, the foreman, found the body about half past five on Wednesday morning as he was going to work. The head was several feet away from the body. The inquest was held on the following Saturday at the Railway hotel in Woking but nothing more was discovered about the victim. Although the evidence suggested suicide, the jury returned an open verdict as it was not clear how the deceased came to be on that part of the line.

Hero or villian?

On 16 March Thomas Henry Prestige – a Salvation Army captain in the Woking branch – drew crowds to hear him preach. He held his meeting on the corner of Chertsey Road and Commercial Road. Unfortunately the police decided he was obstructing the highway and prosecuted him.

Taken to court, he was ordered to pay a fine but refused to do so. An application was made to seize his goods but when the court officials attempted to do this, they discovered that Captain Prestige had given away all his property and there was nothing that could be taken. The captain himself had gone to Brighton.

The magistrates sentenced him to seven days in prison and ordered Inspector Upfold of Woking police to travel to Brighton and escort the runaway back. Captain Prestige served his sentence in Wandsworth prison and, on his release, was regarded as a hero by the people of Woking who paraded him around the town.

Census taken

The census taken during this year showed that the population of Woking was 18,349 and they occupied 2,807 houses.

1902

Unusual funeral

In January a strange procession wended its way from Chertsey to Horsell. Richard Brettell (55), a solicitor, had died on 14 January. He had requested that his coffin, covered by a purple pall, be carried to the church on a farm wagon driven by his employees. Residents turned out to watch the strange procession on its way to Horsell where Mr Brettell had previously lived.

The funeral service was held in St Mary's Church in Horsell and the vicar officiated. Employees of the Grange estate bore the coffin into the church and it was followed by a number of mourners including the sons of the deceased. After the service the remains were reverently laid in the family vault next to Laura, his widow, who had died on 17 January 1885 – almost exactly seven years to the day before her husband. She was only thirty-seven years old.

United in death

A few days later on the morning of Sunday, 19 January a porter at Woking station made a gruesome discovery. The early morning train from Waterloo to Portsmouth stopped at Woking and the porter – a Mr Vidler – noticed there was a hole in one of the windows of a second-class compartment. He assumed that a stone had been thrown until he noticed glass on the step board suggesting that the window had been broken from the inside. When he peered into the carriage he could see nothing as the glass was cloudy, and so he opened the door. He was shocked by what he saw.

A woman was kneeling on the floor; her left arm, resting on the seat, was covered in blood. Opposite her, a man lay on the seat, his face also dripping blood. There was a great deal of blood in the compartment. Ascertaining that both were still alive, the porter hurriedly closed the door and summoned help. The station ambulance arrived promptly and the pair were driven to the Victoria cottage hospital. The man died on the way but the woman survived for two hours after being admitted.

When the police examined the compartment, a small revolver and a bag of cartridges were found. There was no sign of a struggle and it appeared that the deceased had taken their own lives. An inquest was held the following Tuesday at the Albion hotel and the sad story was pieced together.

Henry Scott was a naval pensioner who also kept a tobacconist's shop in Portsmouth. He was forty-five and married with two children. Annie Cooper, who was twenty-nine, was single and lived with her widowed mother in the same town. The two had been friendly for some time and their relationship was generally known about in the town. But things were not going smoothly and both were deeply unhappy.

The coroner and jury heard moving letters that Scott had written to his wife, Lillie, just before he ended his life:

> I have only been a worry to you for the past ten years, ruined your happiness and turned your hair white. I am now leaving you to battle with the world but thank God, both your children are old enough to be able to work for you, which I am sure they will do. . . . My brain is becoming addled. I have felt it coming on for some time now, and I think it is time that the life of hypocrisy I have been leading has made it so. Hence my leaving you . . . I am not leaving alone. The source of all your worry is accompanying me, so I hope that when you have got over the first start, you will soon settle down to spend the remaining days of your life far happier than you have spent those with your unworthy, miserable husband.

The second letter was written in the train just before the fatal shots:

> I am giving Annie her opportunity. I have spoilt her life. She has mine at her disposal. A life for a life. It is only fair. Do not blame her but me.

Annie Cooper had also written to her mother:

> I am writing to ask your forgiveness for the thing I am about to do. Life under the existing circumstances is intolerable to me. I am leaving this world with the only man I have ever loved. I have tried to conceal my real feelings from the world and God knows I have tried hard in the past to crush out all love for him, but I cannot.

At the bottom, Scott had added,

> I can only ask your forgiveness for our sin. Your Annie, or mine, is my all, and I cannot live without her.

From this it was obvious that a suicide pact had been agreed and on Saturday morning, before leaving for London, Scott bought the revolver that would eventually be used to such devastating effect. Later he bade his wife and daughter an affectionate farewell knowing he would never see them again. By midday on Sunday both he and Annie Cooper were dead. It appeared that the wounds had been self-inflicted although it was possible that Cooper might have fired one of the shots at Scott. This would support his comment: 'A life for a life' as he 'had spoilt her life'.

The jury needed only ten minutes to reach their verdict of 'wilful murder'. The following day the couple were buried in one grave in Brookwood cemetery after a short service. Surprisingly, a wreath on Henry Scott's coffin was from 'his sorrowing wife, Lillie'.

Peace at last

At five o'clock in London on a Sunday morning in June the Boer War ended. But the word did not reach Woking for several hours, when it was announced by a railway guard. Unfortunately it came too late to be announced at morning services. Because of poor communication, it was not until Monday morning when the daily papers were delivered that the news became generally known.

A railway porter named Powell appointed himself the town crier. Dressed in an appropriate costume, and carrying one of the station bells, he marched around the town stopping at street corners. After ringing the bell, and shouting out in stentorian tones the traditional 'Oyez, oyez', he announced to the crowds that King Edward VII had commanded him to read a message announcing that the war had ended. There was great rejoicing.

Church bells rang and all school pupils were given a half-day holiday. The wildly excited children flocked around the town waving flags, blowing trumpets and making a noise with any other instruments they could find. Bunting appeared miraculously in the streets and the residents patriotically adorned themselves with anything that was red, white and blue. Bicycles also were decorated with tricolour ribbons and even dogs and cats wore the colours around their necks.

In the evening, Woking was ablaze with lights. Fairy lights twinkled with the words, 'Peace with honour', and even crowns outlined in lights were in evidence outside some residences. In St John's a royal salute was fired by those residents who owned guns. Later there was a torchlight procession through the town and the euphoria lasted well into the night.

Return of the heroes

Later that month a ceremony was held in Guildford to welcome home volunteers from the Queen's Royal West Surrey Regiment. For the past fourteen months they had been fighting in the Boer War and were relieved to be home. A number of the volunteers came from Woking. They were welcomed by a large crowd as a volunteer band struck up 'Soldiers of the King'.

Unlicensed play

On 28 July Sergeant Arney, walking his beat in Church Street, noticed that a large wooden structure with a canvas roof had been erected in an adjoining field. Intrigued, he made his way to it and discovered that the 'building' housed a temporary theatre and that a play, *Lost in London*, was being performed. He watched the play with an audience of over 100 people who had paid either three pence or six pence for the privilege.

Then, remembering the law, he sought out the proprietor, Henry Robert King, who was also one of the actors, and enquired if a performance licence had been obtained. Mr King said that he did not think one was required as the play had been running for about a month. Had he known, he would have applied for one. The police sergeant assured him that no travelling theatre company could perform plays in Woking without a licence and that he would be fined.

Two days later Mr King applied for a licence but the council refused to grant it and took him to court where he pleaded not guilty on the grounds that the play had been 'only a sketch'. The magistrates were not impressed and fined him forty shillings. He was also warned that he might be liable for a £10 penalty for every performance that had been given.

1903

Sergeant attacked by private

One Sunday evening 28-year-old Sergeant Edwin Levy of the first battalion of the Royal Berkshires was savagely attacked by Private William Baxter of the same regiment. The incident took place at Inkerman Barracks. It was after ten at night and Sergeant Levy had just completed the roll call and was walking along the veranda to his room when the private leapt on him and slashed at his face and head with a razor.

Levy shouted for help and other soldiers came to his rescue. Baxter was a powerfully built man, and it was a frenzied attack, so it was some time before they could wrest the weapon from him. Levy had lost a great deal of blood and was taken to the military hospital. Although his condition was critical for a while, his strong constitution helped him to recover quickly.

Baxter was arrested, taken to the guardroom and charged with attempted murder. Having appeared in court, he was remanded in custody until 4 March when it was hoped Sergeant Levy would be well enough to testify.

Silver screen

Woking's first cinema was opened in Chertsey Road by Henry Quartermaine. It seated 150 people and was known as the Central Halls cinema. On one occasion, when a cattle market was being held in Woking, one of the farmers lost a cow. It was eventually located in the balcony of the cinema and had to be coaxed back to join the rest of the herd!

Royal visit

In May the Prince and Princess of Wales spent a weekend at Clandon Park as guests of the Earl and Countess of Onslow. Although it was a private visit, local residents were determined to make the most of it and crowds turned out to welcome them at Clandon station, which had been decorated in their honour.

As they arrived, the band struck up, rather inappropriately, Sousa's march, 'The Stars and Stripes Forever'. It had been expected they would play 'God Bless the Prince of Wales'. The Prince seemed unperturbed as he and his wife set off to Clandon Park with their hosts. The entrance to the park had also been gaily decorated and a flag bearing the feathers of the Prince of Wales had pride of place.

On the Sunday the royal couple joined worshippers for the morning service in West Clandon church and the following day crowds again gathered to watch them leave for London.

All's well that ends well

Pyrford Lock bridge is very narrow and a resident was startled one evening to discover a pair of horses standing nonchalantly near it. There was no sign of the owner. As he got closer, he realised that the animals were attached to a van that had apparently collided with the fence causing one of the wheels to become entangled with the post.

Suspecting that the driver was having a drink at the nearby Anchor Inn, the man went to find him. However, when no driver could be found, the alarm was raised as it was felt that he might have been thrown into the water by the impact. The river was dragged but nothing was found and the search was abandoned until the morning. The van was disentangled from the post and it and the horses were driven back to the owner – a Pyrford tradesman who was naturally afraid something had happened to his driver. However, to everyone's relief, at about eleven o'clock that night, the man turned up at his home apparently none the worse for his adventure.

1904

An impressive funeral

In the early hours of 7 May, Captain Robert Swinton, a well-respected officer of the Royal Berkshire Regiment, died suddenly in his quarters at Inkerman Barracks. It was a great shock to everyone, including his wife, who was herself seriously ill and unable to attend his funeral.

Because of the sudden death, an inquest was held but the jury had no hesitation in determining that Captain Swinton had died of natural causes. His funeral was held the following Tuesday and residents witnessed a most impressive military funeral.

The cortège left Inkerman Barracks just before half-past two. It was headed by a firing party and a Lieutenant Hunt led the escort. The band with their muffled drums followed and then came a gun carriage bearing the coffin draped in a Union Jack; on this lay the captain's sword, which was almost hidden under the wealth of floral tributes. The mourners, including the rest of the battalion, brought up the rear.

At the lychgate of St Mary's, the parish church of Horsell, the procession was greeted by Reverend Ensell, chaplain at Inkerman Barracks, and the deceased's brother officers acted as pallbearers. As the chaplain led the way to the graveside where the funeral service was to be held, the band played Beethoven's 'Funeral March'. The impressive funeral ended appropriately with the 'Last Post'.

1905

A tragic death

At about ten o'clock on the morning of 19 January, Florence Sewry, a housemaid who worked for Miss Roland of Grove Bars, Horsell, heard a scream coming from the kitchen. She rushed down to find the cook, 30-year-old Ellen Bennett, with flames leaping from the back of her clothes. She had been standing in front of the fire and her flannelette underskirt caught fire. Strangely her outer garment had not burned as much. Flannelette was known to be one of the most inflammable materials.

Florence rushed to get her mistress and together they rolled Ellen in a rug to smother the flames and then helped her to bed before calling the doctor. Over the next few days her condition worsened and she was moved to the Royal Surrey County Hospital as there were no beds available at the Woking Victoria Hospital. She died three days later and at the inquest the jury returned a verdict of accidental death.

'Public-house loafer'

On 24 January a Dr Caldicott visited a caravan parked on Lambert's Field in Horsell. It measured only eight and a half feet by five feet and yet it housed five people – two adults and three children. The adults were Walter and Mary Stanley and their three children were 12-year-old Eleanor, Walter, a year younger, and Mabel who was eight. The doctor was horrified by what he found.

The caravan was in a filthy state and the family slept on two shelves hidden behind a curtain. The children were scantily clad and verminous. As a result of the doctor's report, they were removed from their parents' care and taken to the workhouse in Chertsey; Mr and Mrs Stanley were arrested for neglecting them.

Later at the Chertsey Petty Sessions, Walter Stanley was described as a 'public-house loafer' who did no work. The caravan had been lent to the Stanleys by gypsies who camped nearby. No rent was paid but Mary Stanley cleaned for her 'landlords' in return for the use of the caravan. She apparently had no time left to do her own cleaning.

The Stanleys pleaded guilty to the charge of neglecting their children and were sentenced to three months' hard labour.

A drunk lady

Sarah Huntingdon was fined ten shillings by the county bench at Woking for being drunk in Chobham Road on 28 January. She appeared before the bench sporting a bandage over one eye and told the magistrate that the policeman who arrested her had hit her.

Constable Pursey vehemently denied this saying that the defendant had cut her eye when she was 'rolling about in the footway in Chobham Road'. She had fallen into the gutter and, in spite of the help of passers-by, kept falling down. In the end the policeman had to get a truck to wheel her to the station.

Death of an eccentric

George Rastrick, one of Woking's best-known residents, died on 12 April at his home, Woking Lodge. He had only been ill for a few days and was mourned by a widow, two daughters and a son. He had lived in Woking for nearly thirty years and was a wealthy property-owner. In the 1850s he had bought forty acres of land on the south side of Woking station from the Necropolis Company. It had been suggested that he bought the land to prevent anyone developing the town in the direction of Woking Village (Old Woking). Consequently the town developed on the north side of the station. (This accounts for the fact that the main station entrance faces Oriental Road and the back entrance is the one on the town side.)

Regarded as an eccentric, Rastrick lived a secluded life although those who knew him well described him as being 'a great conversationalist'. He left his hermit-like existence on at least one occasion. He had allowed gypsies to camp on his land and Woking Urban Council considered that the encampment had 'become a nuisance dangerous to health' and decided to prosecute them. Rastrick, a solicitor by profession, stoutly defended the gypsies in person in court but lost the case.

By his death Woking lost one of its most influential residents. His funeral took place in Brighton. His coffin, on which were the simple words 'George Rastrick died April 12th 1905', was taken by road to Guildford and then by rail to Brighton central station. From there it travelled to the Extra Mural cemetery where a service was conducted by the chaplain of the cemetery. His coffin was then placed in the family vault where his brother was also buried.

Queen Victoria memorial

At the west end of the town, near the railway arch, a small park was laid out in memory of the late Queen who had died in 1901. It was appropriately named Victoria Gardens.

1906

Barn blaze

On the afternoon of 25 February a group of young men were strolling down White Rose Lane. They were bored and ripe for mischief. When they noticed a barn about twenty yards from the road, they decided to go and investigate. As it was old – and rather dilapidated – they decided to 'knock it about a bit'. Then one of them, Earnest Wheeler, had a better idea. He struck a match and threw it on to the thatch, which immediately caught fire.

The barn belonged to John Wainwright and the damage amounted to £100. Wheeler was later charged with arson. He told the court that he didn't try to put out the fire or fetch the police because the barn 'was such an old place'. The judge sarcastically enquired if all old places should be burned down.

The prisoner was found guilty but the jury felt it was a case of 'boyish mischief' and not 'malice'. He was sentenced to four days' imprisonment.

The scissor-grinder's daughter

A scissor-grinder called Lancaster lived in a tent on the canal bank in Woking because he couldn't afford rent. Asked if it wasn't rather damp, he answered, 'I have a cold bath every morning!' In September he was summoned before the Guildford Board of Guardians whose function was to oversee the welfare of children in the area.

A 13-year-old girl, who claimed to be Lancaster's daughter, had travelled alone from Macclesfield to Woking in search of her father. Lancaster told the board that he had relinquished the care of his daughter to a family in Macclesfield who promised to educate her and 'see to her altogether'. He'd signed a document to that effect in front of a solicitor but had not been given a copy of it.

As he only earned one and sixpence a day, he objected to having to pay towards the upkeep of his daughter but eventually agreed to contribute one shilling per week towards her maintenance in a local children's home. The board decided there was no question of returning her to Macclesfield and Lancaster was warned that if he removed the girl from the home and forced her to live with him in the tent, the NSPCC would become involved.

Romany weddings

In December there were ten weddings in as many days in St Peter's church, Old Woking. It was unusual to have so many in such a short space of time but it was even more unusual to have Romany or gypsy weddings in the church at any time. Romanies had their own ceremonies and rarely darkened the doors of a church.

But the vicar, Reverend Oliphant, and one of his lady parishioners, were very concerned about the gypsies who were camped near Kingfield and visited them regularly. It took a great deal of persuasion to get Romany couples to regularise their unions but eventually the vicar and his helper succeeded, although not without difficulty. It took three attempts before one bridegroom brought his bride to the altar. The couples varied in age from twenty to fifty-five and there were even two generations of one family who were married. On one occasion three couples were married at the same time. The vicar performed the ceremonies free of charge and provided the witnesses.

The last wedding was held on 19 December and all the newly married couples were invited to a tea to celebrate their new status.

Showing off

Thursday, 20 December was show day in Woking. It was the first occasion on which the Tradesmen's Alliance had designated a day on which all tradesmen could display their goods and enhance their business. Although the weather was dull and not at all 'Christmassy', the day was a success. The shops all stayed open late and crowds thronged into the town to search for Christmas presents or to find something extra to add to the pleasure of the day. Mr Wasley, the butcher in Chertsey Road, ordered eight tons of beef to cater for the Christmas demand and he also had a fine display of turkeys and geese.

1907

Sea of mud

For some time an encampment of about ninety gypsies, living in forty tents and caravans, had been occupying land in Well Lane, Horsell, owned by Earnest Lambert, a carpenter, to whom they paid rent. However, the authorities were not happy. Chertsey Rural District Council, which was responsible for the area, had already ordered Lambert to 'abate' the 'nuisance' on his land but he had ignored their instructions.

The 'nuisance' was caused by the state of the ground. Because of wet weather, the land was a slough of mud mixed with excreta from both humans and animals. There were only five 'closets', which the council were responsible for emptying, and the contents had flowed out of them onto the surrounding area. Cesspits from nearby houses had also overflowed onto the land. It was very unpleasant and the council had been concerned for some time.

Dr Brind, the medical officer of health – who had visited the site several times – considered that the field was filthy and a health hazard. The gypsy children had to wade barefoot through the mire to reach their tents. A policeman reported that, when he had visited the camp, the mud almost reached his knees. It was, he said, revolting.

Lambert was summoned to appear before the magistrates at Chertsey, where he was again ordered to 'abate' the 'nuisance' and ensure that it did not happen again. He was fined £2. Mr Thomas Noakes, the relieving officer, told the court that in his twenty-three years of visiting gypsy camps, he had never seen anything like it; horses, dogs and cats roamed freely over the ground, which was covered with filth of all kinds including rabbit skins. The magistrates ordered that the land should be cleansed and the number of people living on it reduced.

Hooligans

During January a group of six errand boys terrorised Horsell. They became known as 'the hooligan gang'. It was the same gang that had damaged the barn in White Rose Lane the previous February for which the ringleader, Earnest Wheeler, had been jailed. They did not appear to have learned their lesson. Hurtling around the village on their bicycles, they showed little concern for other cyclists or pedestrians. At this time Horsell was lit by only one public lamp so the streets were dark and residents preferred to stay indoors rather than risk a confrontation with one of the hooligans. If women were out at night, they would often call on the local policeman, Constable Mann, to escort them home as they were afraid of walking alone through the deserted village.

But one night the gang went too far. Robert Goodyear, who lived in Horsell, was out walking one evening with his young lady, Gertrude Clay, when Wheeler flashed by on his bicycle, which had no lights, and gave a piercing whistle. He then followed the couple into the drive of a nearby house. As he struck Robert Goodyear on the jaw, the rest of the gang appeared and joined in. Gertrude also received a blow on her ear.

Fortunately the owner of the house heard the disturbance and opened the front door, causing the gang to flee. This time Wheeler, and another of the boys, Gibson, were charged with assault. They were sentenced to a month's hard labour in prison. The other members of the gang were each fined twenty shillings but were given the alternative of fourteen days in prison.

Church reopened

In October a large congregation attended a service in Christ Church to celebrate its reopening after renovations costing £2,300. Changes had been made to the north and south transepts, the choir and clergy vestries and the organ chamber. There was also extra seating for 150 people.

Brooklands opened

Hugh Locke King, who owned the huge Brooklands estate, was a motor-racing fanatic; however, he could not enjoy his hobby in England as the country did not have a suitable track. He had to go abroad where races were held on the open roads and spectators were able to see little of the action.

Locke King decided that it was time England got involved in this new and exciting sport. He decided to build a track, which would not be on the highway, and therefore would be safe for spectators who would also see more of the races. He had ample land and planned the circuit very carefully on his Brooklands estate.

He designed a large, oval motor-course where cars could speed and spectators would have a good view in complete safety. It took 1,500 men nine months to complete the track, which was three and a half miles long. It cost £150,000 and was opened on 17 June with the first race being run on 6 July. The track was not restricted to cars. On 8 September, fifty riders took part in the first bicycle race. It was won by J. H. Bishop, who cycled the hundred miles in just under five hours.

Also built for the opening of the track was the clubhouse, known as 'the Weighing Block', because it contained a weighbridge; cars were handicapped by weight in the same way as horses. There were also changing rooms for drivers and offices for stewards.

First car

There was great excitement at the Goldsworth Arms in Goldsworth Road when Mr Whetman, the landlord, became one of the first people in Woking to own a motor car. With a Mr Ireland he bought a DeDion car for £17 from Godwin Brothers and Woking residents were able to see this smart car ambling along the roads at the statutory twenty miles per hour or less.

1908

Turn-up for the Cards

Woking's football team, the Cardinals, known locally as the 'Cards', reached the last sixty-four of the FA Cup. They were the only amateur team left and their tie was against Bolton Wanderers, one of the best sides in the country. It was played at Burnden Park, Bolton's ground. Cardinals' supporters paid thirteen shillings to travel on a special midnight train to Manchester and then to catch another train to Bolton. Woking lost the match by five goals to nil but the visitors played well and had nothing to be ashamed of.

The man in the iron mask

Spectators gaped as a man strode into Woking pushing a perambulator. The fact that he was accompanied by a baby carriage was not what drew the crowds. They were bewildered because he was wearing an iron mask. Was he perhaps impersonating the character in the famous novel by Alexander Dumas? No. He was walking round the world as part of a wager!

An American millionaire, with more money than sense, had put up a wager of $100,000 (about £21,000) if the Englishman could walk round the world pushing the pram, which weighed a hundredweight, and wearing an iron mask. The challenge was accepted and the unusual tour started on 1 January in Trafalgar Square.

To fulfil the conditions of the wager he had to visit North America, New Zealand, Australia, Africa, China, Japan and Europe. In England he had to stop in London, and in each county, before going on to Scotland and Ireland. When he arrived in Woking, he had already journeyed through several counties.

All his expenses had to be met by the sale of postcards and pamphlets describing the wager, and Woking residents were delighted to buy them. He explained that he was not allowed to receive anything free. Everything – even a glass of water – had to be paid for, either in cash or in kind. Hotel bills were saved by travelling with a well-equipped caravan, in which his newly acquired wife rode. Another condition of the wager was that he had to find a wife on the way.

He had taken on an almost impossible task. Whether he won the wager is not known.

Theatre closed

In September the Empire theatre in Duke Street was abruptly closed by the authorities. The theatre was a travelling one and had been erected on wasteland in Duke Street at the end of June. It was about sixty-five feet long and thirty feet wide with boarded sides and a canvas roof. The proprietor, Mr T. E. Little, had applied for a licence but it was refused by the Urban District Council. He then decided that, as a 'strolling player', he didn't need to be licensed.

However, the authorities thought otherwise and on 2 September he was summonsed for having acted in a stage play in an unlicensed theatre. In spite of the fact that the play had been playing to full houses for the past three months, the theatre was closed.

Little pleaded not guilty to the charge and said that he had eighteen people in his company and they depended on him for work; the bench was not impressed. He was fined twenty shillings, with nineteen shillings costs, and warned that he was also liable to a penalty of £10 for every day he had performed in an unlicensed theatre.

Firsts at Brooklands

During this year Malcolm Campbell started his long association with Brooklands and the year also saw three firsts at the circuit. The first ladies' motor-car race was won by Ethel Locke King, the wife of the owner. On 25 February the first motorcycle race was held. The two contenders were W. G. McMinnies on his three horsepower Triumph and O. L. Bickford riding a five horsepower Vindec T. T. Special. The winner was W. G. McMinnies. Following this, on 20 April, twenty-one riders took part in the first official motorcycle race, which was won by W. Cook who averaged sixty-three miles per hour over the two laps.

Brooklands not only catered for motor-car and bicycle enthusiasts but was also the birthplace of British aviation. During the previous year A. V. Roe had been experimenting with planes and conducting trials. He made the first flight from Brooklands on 8 June.

Heavy snowfall

The year closed with the heaviest snowfall for many years, on Monday, 28 December. In places it was up to eight inches deep. Streets were deserted and shops closed early. The railway timetable was disrupted and a football match in which Woking was to have played Windsor in the Oxford Hospital Cup competition had to be cancelled. Because of the depth of the snow, it was some time before it was cleared and people could again go about their daily business.

Low death-rate

According to a report from the medical officer there had been a 'remarkably low death rate' in Woking during 1908.

1909

Fog disrupts

On 25 January, Woking was blanketed in fog and, as the evening drew near, it became even denser. Staying indoors was the best thing to do but Mr Steadman – a carrier who operated between Woking, Send and Pyrford – made the mistake of venturing out in his horse-drawn van. Unfortunately the ditch at the side of the road between Chertsey Bridge and Woodham had recently been cleaned. Unable to see because of the fog, the horse plunged in and broke its neck. Mr Steadman was devastated at the loss of the animal as he depended on it for his livelihood.

A telegraph boy was also on his rounds and he, too, fell into a ditch and lost consciousness. Fortunately he was found and was not badly hurt. The fog caused other problems. The trains were disrupted, and a football match at Inkerman Barracks had to be postponed as it was impossible to see the other side of the pitch.

Away in a manger

On 12 February William and Rose Glue appeared before Woking magistrates. They were charged with neglecting their three children: Emma, twelve, Violet, ten, and William, six.

Inspector James Russell of the NSPCC told the court he had visited a barn on Bannister farm in Artington and found evidence that the family had been sharing the accommodation with a herd of cows. There were indentations in the straw where the parents and children had slept and there was a pile of dirty and verminous clothes. Apparently the family had lived in the barn for about five weeks after being evicted from a cottage because they kept neither it, nor themselves, clean.

After the arrest of their parents, the children were put in the Guildford workhouse. Their hair had to be cut off because of lice and they were bathed twice before they were clean. After the case, William Glue joined his children in the workhouse but his wife had left them.

Schoolboy sues council

In March, Surrey County Council was sued by Alfred Ching, a Woking tailor, on behalf of his 9-year-old son, Cecil, a pupil at Maybury School. Cecil and another boy were in the playground when some older boys decided to chase them. As he ran away Cecil caught his foot in a hole, which was at least four inches deep. He fell over and badly fractured his arm.

Mr Ching considered that Surrey County Council had been negligent in not filling in the hole which, with others, had been a danger for at least six months. In its defence the council put the blame on the local authority in Woking. Albert Clinton, a manager at the school, said he had not been aware of the holes as the premises were examined only once a year. Mr St Gerards, the prosecuting counsel, felt it was very unfair of Surrey County Council to ignore their responsibilities as it was they who had the money and not the local authority.

Arthur Ching testified that he had been put to great expense because of his son's injuries as the boy could no longer run errands for him. The jury decided that Cecil's injuries had been caused by the council's negligence and assessed the damages at over £80.

Orphanage officially opened

On 5 July the Duchess of Albany officially opened the London and South Western Railway Servants orphanage in Oriental Road. The orphanage had originally been founded in 1885 in Clapham by a small group of local railwaymen under the leadership of canon Allen Edwards. In 1907 the company had purchased seven and a half acres of land from the London Necropolis Company at Woking for £2,900. The original orphanage had expanded and more land was required. It was felt that the children would benefit from the country air. The foundation stone of the new building had been laid on 1 October 1907 by the Duchess of Albany.

The orphanage was not always a happy place and there was considerable friction among the staff, some of whom were quite unsuited to their jobs. There was a high turnover of staff and sometimes even the master and matron – often husband and wife – stayed for only a short time. Some were asked to leave because of misbehaviour and one master resigned because he objected to ladies being 'connected with the Management of the Orphanage'. Another man on the committee complained of the ladies' 'lack of business methods and lack of unity'. The ladies, naturally, did not take kindly to this criticism and this caused more unpleasantness. Another couple were asked to resign because of friction among the staff and yet another master was discovered to be 'not quite right in the head'. Other staff were dismissed for drunkenness.

In June 1909 one matron had had enough of the unpleasantness and poor organisation. She complained vociferously and to the committee's horror described the staff as 'scum of the gutter' and the children as 'little scavengers'. She threatened to write to the *Daily Telegraph*. Not surprisingly she was asked to resign, but in spite of the problems, the official opening still took place the following month.

1910

Double bigamy

In January, Ellen Louisa Weston, who was in service in Woking, appeared at Woking Police Court charged with bigamy – not once, but twice! On 4 June 1901 she had married Arthur James Weston at Christ Church. Then on 5 October 1908 at St Mary's church, Horsell, she married James Edward Holmes, a bricklayer. She had told him she was a widow and that her name was Lock.

Having tired of her second 'husband', she then married Harold Blake, a carpenter, on 12 November 1909 at the Congregational church in Guildford. She had told him her name was Phyllis Nellie Weston and that she was single. Eventually the truth came out and she admitted to Blake that she was already married. She promised to leave him but, when she showed no signs of doing so, he informed the police, who arrested her and brought a charge of bigamy.

Blake did some research and produced the certificate of her first legal marriage to Arthur Weston and her second bigamous one to James Holmes, for which she had used a different name. He also showed the court his own marriage certificate. The magistrates were prepared to release her on bail, which was set at £20, but her father refused to stand bail for her 'under any circumstances'. To save face, Ellen said she didn't want bail and she was remanded in custody before being committed for trial at the assizes.

Wanted down under

In March an advertisement appeared in the *Woking News and Mail*:

> *Queensland Australia*
> £5 assisted passages for farmers, farm labourers and agriculturalists. Free passage to wives and children.
> Free passages for female domestic servants. Government takes charge of emigrants until they obtain employment.

A day at the races

On Easter Monday a crowd of about 11,000 gathered at Brooklands to watch the motor racing. The motorcycle races also proved popular. There were fifty entrants and Mr H. Martin won the first race, averaging over fifty-three miles per hour. The second race was won by Mr H. Colier, who averaged sixty-three miles per hour.

But the main draw of the day was the aeroplane flights. Unfortunately these were not a success. During the afternoon two flying machines were brought out of their sheds but did not justify their appearance. As the *Woking News and Mail* informed its readers, the aeroplanes 'made attempts to fly but their existence in the air was short lived'.

Trigger happy

In April, a tragic event occurred in the household of Mr Kenneth Wilson of the Patch, Hookheath. Maggie Ford, a kitchen maid, and Alice Randall, a housemaid, were in the pantry making up a bed for Harry Shaw, a footman who slept in the pantry. It was where the silver was stored and, because he was on guard, he kept a gun in the drawer beside his bed.

While Alice and Maggie were making the bed, the 16-year-old house boy, Richard Uttridge, came into the room. Seeing the gun in the open drawer and assuming it was unloaded, he picked it up and, pointing it at Alice, said jokingly, 'Hands up!'

She laughed and he pulled the trigger. To his horror, Alice collapsed on the floor. The gun was loaded and she had been shot in the head. Maggie screamed and rushed out of the room to fetch help. The victim was taken to the cottage hospital but an operation to remove the bullet was not successful and she died.

At the inquest, the coroner described it as a 'sad case'. He spoke strongly about the need to keep guns secure but concluded that the tragedy had been an unfortunate accident. Richard Uttridge left the court weeping bitterly.

Plane crazy

The speed limit for cars at this time was twenty miles per hour and the authorities were vigilant in enforcing it. It was not difficult to catch offenders and they were usually fined. However, in the air, there was no speed limit and one of those charged with breaking the speed limit on the road took full advantage.

Brooklands motor-racing circuit had also given birth to British aviation; on 21 May crowds gathered in a field near the circuit to watch Claude Grahame-White climb into his Farman biplane and take off for Westfield, where he was due in court charged with speeding. The farmer who owned the field had taken advantage of the unusual event and charged each onlooker sixpence for the privilege of watching.

In Westfield, the magistrates fined Mr Grahame-White £5 for breaking the law and charged him eight shillings and sixpence costs. Having paid his dues, the intrepid flyer boarded his plane again and flew off, to the delight of the Westfield residents who had come to watch. Even the magistrates had no intention of ignoring this historic event and also gazed skywards as the biplane became a mere speck in the sky.

The pilot had obtained his flying licence earlier the same year; he was the first Englishman to do so. He then started a school of aviation at Brooklands and in April made aviation history when he raced his plane from London to Manchester against Louis Paulham. But it was his flight to answer his summons for speeding that made him famous in Woking.

Floods

There was severe flooding at the end of the year and the main street in Old Woking was covered in two feet of water. Some houses were cut off with their gardens submerged and the water battering at the doors. A few were flooded, forcing the occupants to retreat upstairs with their possessions and collect provisions through the upper windows.

Children at the Church Street school were delighted to be given a half-day holiday and employees at the nearby Unwin's printing works were sent home at three-thirty in the afternoon, instead of six o'clock, because of the rising water. It was impossible for pedestrians to walk or cyclists to cycle. The few motor cars, too, had problems as water seeped into the engines, causing them to stall.

Other conveyances were used to ferry pedestrians. One cyclist, being carried through the village on a milk float, fell off into the water but sustained no injury. It was not the first time passengers had to be ferried through Old Woking. A former employee of Unwin's, Benjamin Pitter, had often helped residents through the village when it was flooded. During the latest floods, at the age of seventy-five, he died, and was ferried through the water to his grave.

1911

Ladies take the plunge

Woking District Council decided that, on two mornings each week, the swimming pool should be set aside for the exclusive use of ladies. Mixed bathing was popular in Walton but it had not yet been tried in Woking. One correspondent had written to the *Woking New and Mail* suggesting that it should be introduced. He pointed out that it had been so successful in Walton that it continued throughout the year and not just in the summer.

Census taken

In the ten years since 1901 the population of Woking had increased by over 6,000. The number of people living in Woking when the census was taken in 1911 was 24,810.

First ticket office

Brooklands again led the way. A flight ticket-office was built and opened. This was the forerunner of the airport terminal and the first of its kind. It was run by Keith Prowse & Co. and, for a few guineas, passengers could experience the thrill of a short flight in one of the new machines.

The Woking poltergeist

During May the family of Mr Holroyd, who lived in a house on the outskirts of Woking, was disturbed by unearthly shrieks and wails coming from their hall, which was surrounded by a balcony at first-floor level. The house was modern, standing in its own grounds, and seemed an unlikely habitation for ghosts. But there was no other explanation.

The maid first heard the screeching one Thursday morning. She was terrified and rushed to get her master. By the time he arrived, the noise had stopped and he said it was just her imagination. But she refused to stay alone in the kitchen so Mr Holroyd's 12-year-old son was deputed to sit with her. At midday the noise started again and both heard it.

The following Saturday the howling started again as the boy walked past the hall. His father accused him of being responsible but he denied it, and his sister also said she had heard the noise and was frightened. Then the family's bull terrier ran across the hall and stopped in the middle with hair bristling before howling and bolting into the dining room. The children's governess also said she had heard tapping at the window and that bells had rung for no apparent reason. Eventually Mr Holroyd heard the sounds and was forced to believe there was something strange going on.

During the next few days the noise was heard many times. It sounded like a woman crying out in agony and there were also unexplained thuds. Various explanations were put forward but none seemed right and, although the police searched the premises thoroughly, nothing was found.

The press heard about it and reporters were sent round; they also were subjected to the terrifying screeches. Ghost hunters and the curious, attracted by the story, flocked to stare at the house in the hope of hearing something. A number of local residents remembered that a previous occupant of the house had been a medium and suggested this might have something to do with it.

On Saturday, 20 May, for the first time, there were piercing shrieks at night. The next morning the noise started again at midday but to the relief of the family that was the last time the poltergeist was heard. Mr Holroyd was convinced there must have been some rational explanation for the disturbances but none was ever found. It remains one of Woking's greatest mysteries.

Coronation day

Thursday, 22 June was coronation day for His Majesty King George V and Queen Mary. Woking was awash with flags and bunting; a huge Union Jack flew over the council offices and all the shops competed to produce the best window display. Everyone was looking forward to the festivities. The day started with an overcast sky and drizzling rain but fortunately it cleared and hundreds of people thronged the streets.

The first event was a morning service at Christ Church. It was ecumenical and the lessons were read by Reverend Nicholson from the Wesleyan chapel and Reverend Tebbit, the Baptist minister. The service started with the hymn 'Oh God Our Help in Ages Past' and this was followed by prayers for the King and Queen and a sermon from the vicar. The local Boys' Brigade attended the service and afterwards their band paraded through the streets.

Old people were entertained to a dinner in the Public Hall and in the afternoon there was a procession through the town. Headed by the Mayford Industrial School Band, it left the council offices at two o'clock and marched to the recreation ground. The band was followed by children from the local schools carrying banners and waving flags.

At the recreation ground a short address was followed by the planting of five young oak trees near the Constitution Hill entrance to commemorate the day. There were sports events followed by tea and children were presented with coronation medals and mugs. The evening ended with an impressive firework display organised by Mr Evans of Chertsey Road.

1912

Infanticide

On the evening of 22 March, Mary Ann Eldridge of Woking strangled her three young children: Winifred aged four, Freda aged two and Florence who was just fifteen months. The latter's body was still warm when the bodies were found. The mother was quite open about what she had done and told a neighbour that her babies were 'in heaven'. She appeared to have no regrets. She was an alcoholic and the court was told she had been drinking heavily for several weeks before the crime.

Her defence counsel made much of her state of mind at the time. She had been taunted by her common-law husband about her 'bastard' children and she was so upset when he had denied being the father that she decided the children were 'better out of the way'. She had intended to take her own life as well but was arrested before she could do so.

The jury found her guilty of murder but agreed with her counsel that she was insane. Instead of the death penalty, the judge sentenced her 'to be detained as a criminal lunatic at His Majesty's pleasure'.

Murder of a girl scout

Another murder that also shocked the community was that of a 12-year-old, also called Winifred. On 5 December Winifred Baker, a pupil at Goldsworth School, was found dead in a passageway in Walton Road. She had been strangled with her own scarf. The previous evening, after a meeting of the Nightingale Scouts to which she belonged, she had left the mission hall in Walton Road with two other girls. As they walked up the road, they were accosted by a man who told them their teacher needed one of them. Braver than her companions, Winifred went off with him. She was never seen alive again.

Once suspicions were aroused a search was launched but no trace of her, or her abductor, was found. It was not until the next day that her body was discovered in a passage that had been empty the previous evening. As it had been raining, and the girl's clothes were dry, it was clear that she had been murdered elsewhere and her body dumped in the passage. The inquest heard that Winifred's underclothes had been torn and 'an outrage' had taken place.

In spite of an intensive search, the killer was never found and Winifred was buried in Brookwood cemetery on 11 December. Her funeral was attended by 350 of her fellow pupils from Goldsworth and her Nightingale hat, which had been found near her body, was placed on the coffin.

Reopening of the mosque

The Shah Jehan Mosque in Oriental Road reopened its doors in 1912 after having been closed for twelve years. The first mosque to be built in England, it was opened in 1889 to serve the needs of the Muslim students at the nearby Oriental Institute, which had given its name to Oriental Road. The institute and the mosque both closed in 1899.

The mosque remained closed until 1912 when an Indian barrister gave up his practice in India to become the first Muslim missionary to this country. He reopened the mosque and it has served the large Muslim community in Woking ever since.

1913

A cruel con

Fake memorial cards in memory of the murdered Nightingale Scout, Winifred Baker, were being sold for tuppence and Woking residents were warned not to buy them. It was said that the proceeds were to go to the parents, but they denied all knowledge of the cards.

Ton up

At Brooklands, Percy Lambert drove his motor car at a hundred miles per hour – the first driver to do so.

The monster goldfish

Another form of transport caused great excitement one evening. People came out of their homes to watch the new airship *Parsifal* pass over Woking. At 290-feet long and forty-six-feet wide, it had recently been acquired for the Royal Navy and was making its trial run from Farnborough to London and back. It attracted considerable interest as it floated through the air; low enough for spectators to obtain a good view of the 'monster gold fish' as the *Woking News and Mail* described it.

Meeting disrupted

On 12 May, Whit Monday, a public meeting was held on Mayford Green. It was organised by the National Union of Women's Suffrage and the speaker was

Miss Philippa Fawcett, whose mother was one of the leaders of the movement. In spite of the bad weather, crowds had gathered to hear her.

Unfortunately not all of her audience wished to listen. She had just started to speak when an egg was thrown at her; it missed but struck a small girl standing nearby, splattering both the child and her father. Incensed at being covered with egg, he attacked the man who had thrown the missile and a fight broke out. Others joined in, more eggs were thrown and cries of 'down with women' drowned out the speaker who decided not to compete with the noise. She left the platform followed by the organisers. Shortly afterwards a group of students from a nearby training farm drove up in a wagon also intent on disrupting the meeting. They were too late.

Many of the crowd were angry that the meeting had been abandoned as they wished to hear what the speaker had to say on the subject of women's suffrage.

Curtain up

At the end of November the new picture palace at the corner of Duke Street and Maybury Road was opened. The Palace Theatre attracted a large audience at the first matinee and the evening performance was so popular that many people had to stand. The film that was chosen to mark the opening was *The Last Days of Pompeii*, based on the novel by Lord Lytton.

Empire Day

Empire Day was always celebrated on 24 May and in 1913 the day fell on a Saturday, which turned out to be one of the hottest days of the year. Woking was decorated with flags and bunting and crowds turned out to join in the festivities.

At half past two a procession, led by three bands, marched from the council offices to the recreation ground in sweltering heat. Behind the bands came children from the local schools each with a banner at the front. When they arrived at their destination, the children formed a large semi-circle around the platform while the Union Jack was hoisted and the national anthem was played by Mayford School band. This was followed by a prayer for the Empire by Reverend Askwith and the singing of patriotic songs. Unfortunately some of the children, overcome by standing in the heat, fainted and had to be treated in the Red Cross tent.

After the songs, there was a speech, followed by three cheers for the King; then there were sports for the children culminating in a display of maypole dancing. After tea, it was the turn of the adults. The grounds were illuminated and there was dancing to the band of the Royal Sussex Regiment. The evening ended with a spectacular firework display, which included a naval battle.

1914

Death of a pilot

Sergeant Eric Deane, who was twenty-four, was so enthusiastic about flying that, while on leave, he spent all his spare time at Brooklands training to fly at his own expense. During the spring, whenever the weather was fine, he could be found at the aerodrome. At the end of his training he did some test flying under the watchful eye of Frank Wright, an official observer of the Royal Aero Club. The day was perfect for flying, with only a gentle breeze.

Sergeant Deane started his test at half past six in the morning. He completed two tests, which Wright said were the best he had ever seen. Then he started the third, which consisted of five figures of eight at a height of at least 328 feet over a set course. At the end he had to cut out the engine and land in a designated area. As was common, he was not strapped in.

The test went well. The pilot climbed to 1,000 feet and then started a spiral descent at a very steep angle. Then, to the watcher's horror, as the plane hurtled downwards, the pilot was tossed out of the machine. He landed on his back and died instantly; his plane crashed some distance away.

At the inquest held on 9 April it was stated that Deane was an excellent flyer and never reckless. Wright thought the accident was probably due to an error of judgement. The jury brought in a verdict of accidental death but suggested that the pilot should have been strapped into his seat.

War

On 4 August, Great Britain declared war on Germany.

Anti-German feeling

Public feeling grew against anyone with either a German name or any connection with Germany. In September, Thomas Selle, who worked for a Woking nursery, was charged with having a revolver in his possession. He had no permit. For this he was fined £50. It was also noted that he had been boasting that he kept homing pigeons, through which he was able to communicate with Germany. Sulkily, Selle replied that he had been drunk when that remark had been made. The charge was dropped.

A butcher, Ludwig Betz, a German, was sentenced to six months' hard labour because he had not registered as all foreigners had to do. He ran away when questioned and, although fluent in English, refused to answer when questioned in that language. Another man was fined £20 for going beyond the five-mile limit set for aliens.

No conscientious objectors

Conscription was introduced for men over eighteen and under forty-one, but many had a conscientious objection to military service; they had no protection in law and many of those who refused to take up arms were imprisoned.

However, the government was concerned and a committee was set up. As a result, a circular letter was sent to all urban district councils asking if they were prepared to employ conscientious objectors. Woking Urban District Council refused to do so.

As well as conscience, there were other grounds for exemption from military service and local tribunals were set up to hear cases. One such case was that of Robert Williams, a teacher at Goldsworth School. If he were called up to serve his country, the school would be left without any male teachers, a situation the Woking education committee was not happy about as half the pupils in the school were boys. The local tribunal was sympathetic and granted Williams two months' 'conditional and temporary exemption'. A further application would be made if no suitable replacement could be found.

New boys' school

In September the Boys' Secondary School and Institute was opened in Guildford Road with fewer than fifty boys. The land had been bought from the nurseryman, Mr Slocock, four years' earlier. He had originally paid £3,000 for it after George Rastrick died. The first headmaster was Joshua Holden from Yorkshire; he had been selected from 150 applicants from all over the country.

Christmas at the front

A Woking lady received a fascinating letter from her nephew, a private in the sixteenth battalion of the Rifle Brigade. He was serving on the front line but the actual place was not identified for security reasons. He described an historic event:

> We have a good deal to put up with out here but all the fellows, including myself, are exceedingly cheerful about it. We do a good deal of singing; it is a cheering way of spending our unoccupied time as well as when on the march and in the trench. We were in the trenches on Christmas Day and had a unique experience. Both sides came out of their trenches and met in the centre and exchanged greetings. This was not the general thing, I think, as we could hear firing on both sides of us.

Death in a caravan

At the end of the year severe storms caused roads to be flooded. A plate-glass window in a drapery store in Duke Street was blown in and the large arc-lamp outside Woking station was damaged. The hurricane was followed by snow, which lay until heavy rain caused more flooding. In Old Woking a wagonnette was pressed into service to ferry passengers as it was impossible to walk.

The storm also uprooted trees. Onslow Crescent was blocked by large branches and a huge elm at Westfield farm fell on a cart shed, totally destroying it. But the worst disaster was on Mayford Road where a caravan had parked on the grass verge under a large tree for shelter. A violent gust uprooted the tree, which fell on the caravan splintering it to pieces. Elizabeth Jones, a 19-year-old flower seller, was the only occupant and was killed instantly. It took rescue workers four hours to remove her mangled remains from underneath the vehicle.

Her 24-year-old companion, John Hall, and her two younger brothers of fifteen and eighteen, who shared the caravan with her, were not there at the time and the horse was tethered some distance away so poor Elizabeth was the only casualty.

1915

Martinsyde Ltd

In 1915 Martinsydes – which had used the Brooklands site to make and experiment with aircraft – was finally registered as Martinsyde Ltd. The company took over the ten acres of land that had formerly been the site of the Oriental Institute. It was on the corner of Oriental Road and Maybury Hill. They kept the original building but built a new factory in the grounds.

Two men, Helmut Paul Martin and George Harris Hardasyde, had given their names to the company. The combination of 'Martin' and 'syde' made 'Martinsyde'. Both men were engineers and fascinated by aeroplanes. In 1910 they had rented a shed at Brooklands and the first flight of their monoplane had taken place in October of that year. They had managed to fly it 300 yards.

Their new factory in Maybury Hill was far superior and during the war they were able to mass-produce aircraft, eventually becoming the world's third-largest aircraft-manufacturer. After the war, when there was not such a demand for planes, Martinsydes turned to motorcycles, producing over two thousand of them.

Sacred ground

The Great War continued to produce horrors and one issue caused great concern to Indian soldiers – many of whom were Muslims – fighting at the front alongside the British. The German propaganda machine rolled into action and circulated rumours that Indian soldiers who died in England were not being buried with due reverence.

Muslims living in Woking were extremely disturbed by the rumours. So was the British government. It announced that a site should be found for the interment of Muslim soldiers who had died during the war. As the possessor of the only mosque in England, Woking was chosen and the council met to discuss the situation.

At the meeting it was pointed out that a section of Brookwood cemetery was already devoted to Muslim burials, but local Muslims wanted to buy a piece of land near the mosque in Oriental Road for the purpose. This suggestion was rejected by the council because the area was residential and it was felt that locals would object to having a burial ground in their midst.

After much discussion an area of Horsell Common near the Basingstoke canal in Monument Road was chosen and the burial ground was finally erected in 1915. It was designed by architect T. H. Winney and built by a local firm, Ashby & Horner Ltd. Indian soldiers, who were wounded at the Western Front, were brought to Brighton for hospital treatment and many died there. Nineteen soldiers were buried in the Muslim cemetery in graves facing the east, according to Muslim custom.

A celebration

One Friday in August an unusual celebration of the Muslim Festival of Eid took place at the Shah Jehan mosque. It was unusual because among the congregation were fifty Indian soldiers who had been wounded in the war. They were convalescing in New Milton in Hampshire but had been allowed to travel to Woking for this important festival. Many of them had been wounded several times.

Accompanied by two officers, they marched smartly down Oriental Road. Arriving at the mosque, they replaced their khaki uniforms with the traditional white robes worn by Muslim men. Over three hundred people attended including Lord Headley, the president of the British Muslim Society, an Indian prince, an Egyptian princess and a judge from Madras High Court. Also present were some ladies and a number of local converts to Islam.

As the mosque could not accommodate all the visitors, the service was held outside. It was conducted by the Imam, Maulvie Sadr-ud-din, and after the customary Arabic prayers, he addressed the assembled company first in English and then in Hindustani, the language of the wounded soldiers.

Soldier lost his regiment

A soldier charged at Woking Magistrates Court with desertion was found to have been in hospital and then on sick leave. Returning to his barracks, he found that his regiment had returned to the front without him. Not knowing what to do, he wandered around the town until picked up by the Military Police.

'I had no intention of deserting, sir,' he assured the magistrate as he left the court to get his discharge from the army on medical grounds.

1916

Distinguished by bravery

In March, 22-year-old private Joseph Drowley was awarded the Distinguished Conduct Medal. He wrote to his parents, who lived in Maybury Road, saying that while he was, of course, 'very pleased to hear it . . . it came almost as a thunderbolt to me because what I did was only my duty'.

The medal was awarded for his bravery in North Africa in the January. He had fought bravely, and accounted for several Arabs, when he realised that one of his companions was lying wounded about fifty yards from the enemy. He and another soldier crawled towards the injured man and brought him to safety.

Private Drowley had been a pupil at Maybury School and a keen member of the local cricket and football clubs. His army training had been in Guildford and Canterbury and he first went abroad in October 1914.

The curate is appealing

A former curate of Christ Church, Cyril Wilson, now at the front, wrote an appeal to members of the church:

> I have been shifting all over the place . . . as our division has been split up and sent to all parts of the globe. I have had a club for the men handed over to me. I am wanting all sorts of things – magazines, books, games, eatables, – anything and everything will be most acceptable. The club is on the way to the trenches, right among the batteries and it is a great help to the men. Aeroplanes are a nuisance backed by the guns and do their very best to spoil our services in the open air. . . . At present I am billeted in a farm and have a very strong objection to sharing my bedroom with rats but the rats refuse to see it in the same light.

House of ill repute

On 6 September a soldier's wife, Freda Norton, was given two prison sentences by a Woking magistrate for 'keeping a disorderly house' and for allowing her three children to live in the brothel while her husband was serving with the armed forces in Mesopotamia.

Charged with aiding and abetting her, was 15-year-old Rose Spencer. Rose worked in a cigar factory in Guildford and Mrs Norton had agreed with Rose's mother that she would give the girl lodgings and look after her. But instead of caring for the teenager, she encouraged her to lead an immoral life, abusing the trust that had been placed in her. Local residents reported that they had seen Freda Norton and Rose going into the house with a number of different soldiers.

The magistrate said it was one of the worst cases to have come before him. He put Rose Spencer on probation for two years on condition that she returned to live with her mother. Mrs Norton's husband was granted custody of their children and it was understood that he would make arrangements for his parents to look after them while he was overseas. Norton was given a three-month prison sentence for running a brothel and six months for allowing her children to live there. The sentences were to run concurrently.

The great escape

On Monday, 25 September, five German prisoners of war escaped from the Frith Hill internment camp at Frimley and were roaming around the Woking countryside for two days. They had been with a group of prisoners at Pirbright working on the construction of a light railway from Brookwood to Deepcut. However, they eluded their guards and fled. An intensive search, using bloodhounds, was mounted by the military and the police. The following day footprints were found. They were identified as belonging to the prisoners because of the indentation made by large nails on the soles of their boots.

It was on Wednesday morning that Special Constable James, while on his beat in Ascot, discovered three of the prisoners sleeping by the side of the road. They were seven miles from the camp. Exhaustion and hunger had taken their toll and the prisoners made no attempt to evade capture. Two of them were sailors and one was an airman. Their companions remained at large.

1917

Casualties of war

Corporal William Jordan of the Coldstream Guards, from St John's, was first reported missing on 29 October 1914 after being involved in fierce fighting at Ypres. The official news that he was definitely 'missing' was given to his wife in February the following year. But it was not until January of 1917 that Mrs Jordan got her husband's battered identity-disc back. It looked as if it had been dug out of the mud, as indeed it probably had been. Two of Jordan's brothers and his brother-in-law had also been killed.

Every week the *Woking News and Mail* was full of the casualties of the Great War. The post office displayed a roll of honour of those employees who had given their lives and it was noted that the five sons of Mr and Mrs Gibbons from Maybury Hill were all serving overseas.

Napoleon's sword

Mr Hutchinson of Melrose Cottage, Woodham Road, had a reminder of another war. He was the proud owner of a sword that had been given to Napoleon by a brother officer when he received his first commission in 1786 at Valence. It was a French court sword and was inscribed on one side 'A mon ami Mons de Buonoparte' and on the other 'Souvenir 1786 Valence'.

Mr Hutchinson decided that he would sell it at auction and give the proceeds to the Red Cross and the Order of St John. He offered it to Christie's the auctioneers.

A strange request

At a meeting of the Woking Urban Council one of the councillors, Mr J. Strudwick, moved a strange resolution. He suggested 'that the board in the Council Chamber containing the names of the past Chairmen of the Council be re-written omitting the name and years of office of Mr G. F. Wermig'.

Wermig had been the first chairman of the council in 1895. Strudwick declined to give any reasons for his request but insisted that he was carrying out the wishes of the ratepayers by bringing the matter to the council's attention. Another councillor, Mr Golding, seconded the motion and it was opened up for discussion.

It was pointed out that the board was a statement of fact and deleting Mr Wermig's name would not eradicate his three years of office, during which he had done a great deal for the town. He was a well-known market-gardener, but of German birth. As England was at war with Germany, anyone of German extraction was regarded with suspicion and this was probably the reason for Mr Strudwick's strange request. Even the King had changed his name to Windsor from his German family name, Saxe-Coburg.

The council did not agree to the request and one councillor regarded the discussion as 'most unprofitable . . . from every point of view'.

Royal visit

On 27 April King George V and Queen Mary paid an informal visit to Martinsyde's aeroplane works. The Queen was particularly surprised to discover women working in an aircraft factory and spent time chatting to them.

The King was interested to meet the oldest employee of the company – a man named Baker, who was sixty-nine. It transpired that he had been a crew member on the yacht *Osborne* when she cruised up the Baltic in 1864. On board were the King's parents, King Edward VII and Queen Alexandra, who had been married the previous year.

1918

Shakespeare at school

In March, Reg Church, one of the masters at the Boys' Grammar School, directed the school drama group in a production of Shakespeare's *Twelfth Night*. As in Shakespeare's day, the female parts were played by boys and the play was a great success. It was the first of many, and Church directed school plays for many years. A popular tradition had started.

Potato record?

In September Mr Chapman of Russell Road, Horsell, was startled when he harvested his potato crop. One of his 'long keeper' potatoes weighed two pounds, six and a half ounces. It had to be a record.

Tribunals

Throughout the year tribunals were kept busy deciding which men could be legitimately exempted from military service. One disgruntled applicant told the Woking tribunal about a friend of his who had had his exemption refused. During his year in the army, this man had been kept very busy washing plates, digging trenches, pumping water and whitewashing. Was this really more important than letting men carry on their legitimate businesses?

Peace at last

This year heralded the long-awaited peace. At eleven o'clock on the eleventh day of the eleventh month the Great War came to an end and Woking, like the rest of the country, rejoiced. The news reached Inkerman Barracks first on that Monday morning and from there it spread rapidly through the town. A general holiday was declared and cheering crowds thronged the hastily decorated streets waving flags, embracing strangers and congratulating each other. On the balcony of the Albion Hotel opposite the station, Mr Godfrey, chairman of the Urban Council, voiced the feelings of the crowd when he spoke of the relief of the country and the gratitude felt towards those who had died. Other impromptu speeches followed but they were drowned out by the cheers of the people and the enthusiastic playing of the Mayford School Band.

In the afternoon there was a procession through the town and a crowded meeting was held in the Palace Theatre in the evening when Canon Devereux, vicar of Christ Church, gave an address thanking God for victory and remembering those who had given their lives.

For the rest of the week there were services of thanksgiving and other celebrations, culminating in a torchlight procession through the town on Saturday evening. This was followed by a military tattoo on Wheatsheaf Common where an effigy of the Kaiser was burnt on a large bonfire. The celebration ended with a spectacular firework display.

On the Sunday afternoon an unusual meeting of thanksgiving was held in the Palace Theatre to give thanks for the services rendered in the war by the South African Brigade, which had been stationed in Woking. A message had been sent to the King informing him of the meeting and his reply was read to the congregation:

> The King has received with much gratification the message you have addressed to him on the occasion of the mass meeting held at Woking this evening to express gratitude to the South African Brigade stationed at Woking. While I am to assure you that his Majesty's heartfelt sympathy goes out to the bereaved homes, the King warmly rejoices with the people of Woking in their Thanksgiving celebration over the glorious triumph which the Empire's cause has achieved.

1919

First woman councillor

Lady Betty Balfour was the first woman councillor to be elected in Woking. She represented St John's. Her husband was Gerald Balfour, the brother of Arthur James Balfour, who had become Conservative prime minister in 1902.

It was too successful

On New Year's Day a national restaurant opened in Woking – and closed nine days later because it was too popular! The supervisor, Mrs Harcourt Paine, and her staff resigned after giving only a day's notice because they couldn't cope with the number of customers.

Many of the staff were volunteers and Mrs Paine had qualified to run a national kitchen during the war under the food control committee. Most of the staff had trained for war work and did not wish to man an ordinary restaurant during peacetime, even if most of the diners were service personnel.

On the first day sixty-four meals were served. As the place grew in popularity, the number of customers increased and the staff could not keep up. The restaurant could cater for a hundred people but, when her small staff had to serve 158 meals in an hour, Mrs Paine called a halt. The restaurant needed to be managed properly, she told the national kitchen committee. 'It is no undertaking for amateurs,' she said. Sadly, the committee was obliged to close the restaurant. It had certainly been a nine-day wonder.

Is the bread poisoned?

Before the war, millers were allowed to add various chemicals to bread in order to make it as white as possible. This practice was discontinued during the war. In 1916 white bread had been banned; a healthier, darker loaf had been introduced and millers had to use barley, oats, rye, soya or potato flour.

After the war the use of chemicals was again permitted. However, one miller, a Mr Holroyd, was not happy about this. He felt that chemicals could be harmful to health so he decided to experiment. He gave a chemical mixture to a cat, which was never seen again. Suspicious of this, Holroyd gave a similar mixture to his dog, which then became ill. The miller was convinced this was a result of the chemicals. He felt strongly that their use should be banned because he was sure there was a possibility they might cause illness, perhaps even cancer.

Dr Brind, chairman of Chertsey Rural Council, agreed with him that 'there should be no sophistication of foodstuffs' as there had already been too much 'tinkering' with bread. It is not known whether the government took note of the council's recommendation.

Fire brigade's embarrassment

Woking fire brigade had an embarrassing time in June. The crew were routinely pumping out the water from the swimming pool when the steam fire-engine, dating from 1899, collapsed and became, according to the *Woking News and Mail,* 'unserviceable for fire purposes'.

Unfortunately, Dennis Brothers, which provided the brigade with its engines, was unable to give a date for the delivery of a new engine. Lacking the facilities to deal with local fires, Woking had to call on the services of the Guildford brigade, which promised to render assistance if necessary.

The new engine was not delivered until September but it was worth waiting for; it was not only a motor vehicle but also boasted a telescopic ladder. It was put to immediate use as the brigade was called out to quench a small fire that had broken out in a woodshed in Maybury Road. The fire had quickly spread to an overhead storeroom causing the smoke to penetrate the rafters and billow out of the windows. The fire crew were on their way within minutes of receiving the call and used forty gallons of water to extinguish the blaze.

The following day there was a more unusual fire in Goldsworth Road. Red-hot soot from one of the chimneys had settled on the roof setting it alight. Fortunately a passing policeman raised the alarm and the fire was put out using the new chemical-fire-extinguisher. Half an hour after first receiving this call, the firemen were back at the station demonstrating the efficiency of the Woking brigade with its new equipment.

An officer and a gentleman

In November, Lieutenant Henry Forbes – a decorated veteran of the first world war, who had lost a leg in the service of his country – appeared at Woking Police Court charged with assaulting a brother officer's wife.

The wife in question was Mrs Winifred Davies whose husband, a second lieutenant, was Forbes's subordinate. Both served in the Royal Army Medical Corps. Before the alleged assault took place, the two couples had been on friendly terms and there had never been any question of intimacy between Mrs Davies and Lieutenant Forbes.

However, Mrs Davies alleged that the officer assaulted her on 16 October near the RAMC offices where her husband worked. On that evening she had been upset because her husband was late home and she had decided to go to his office to meet him. Near the station she met Forbes who was meeting his wife off the London train. She said he gallantly offered to escort her to her husband's office as she had to walk through a dark alley to the huts where the RAMC were based.

She told the court that, when they reached the area, her companion asked if he could kiss her. When she refused, he dragged her towards the huts and, forcing her up against the side of one of them, started to fumble with her clothing, saying, 'You excite me.' Her glasses were knocked off and two buttons were torn from her coat.

The 'assault' lasted about five minutes and when she eventually escaped, she ran into the hut to find her husband. He was not there so she made several phone calls to track him down. Failing to do so, she went home and, when he returned, she told him what had happened.

Apparently Lieutenant Davies had been in London on that day but had been unable to let his wife know. Forbes admitted he knew this as he had issued his junior officer with a voucher for the ticket; but he strenuously denied that any assault had taken place. His wife corroborated this as she testified that when she arrived at the station from London, she met her husband who had been talking to Mrs Davies and she saw the other woman leave so he could not have walked down the road with her. She said Mrs Davies had often complained about her husband's drinking and staying out late. She described Mrs Davies as 'a very hysterical woman'.

The magistrate, Colonel Phayre, was not impressed by what he had heard. He refused to hear any other witnesses and dismissed the case, leaving Forbes without a stain on his character.

1920

Six to a room

Lack of housing was a major problem. Landlords could be prosecuted if they allowed too many people to occupy one room. Mrs Harriet Jones, who lived in Vale Farm Road, was one such landlord. She had allowed another family, the Youngs, to share her three-bedroom cottage. There were fourteen people living in the small house – eight of her family and six of the Youngs, so six people were sleeping in one room.

Mrs Jones received a summons from the Urban Council because her house was overcrowded; she had to go to court to obtain an order for the Youngs to be evicted from the two rooms they occupied. Her family had the use of only one bedroom. Apparently the downstairs rooms were not in a 'usable condition' as the floor had 'fallen through'. The Youngs' 17-year-old daughter appeared as the defendant and told the court that Mrs Jones had 'no use for the rooms at all' as she had 'no furniture to put there'.

The magistrate smartly reminded her that her landlord had 'some human beings to put there' and ordered her to tell her father that his family must leave Mrs Jones's house within twenty-one days.

Very co-operative

In March, the Co-operative Society opened its fifth store. This was in Monument Hill. It had been a long time in the planning but at last it was ready. The president of the Co-operative Society, Mr Prosser, presided and Woking Town Band entertained the waiting crowd before the ceremony.

The architect, Mr Bethell, presented Mr Savage, the chairman of the management committee, with a silver key. After the shop was declared open, crowds flooded in and then adjourned to Martinsydes factory where tea had been provided.

A quiet drink

A number of gypsies surged into Woking Police Court on Saturday, 10 April, to support one of their number, Horace Willet, who had been charged with attacking Mrs Jane Saunders of South Road, Horsell. She appeared in court with two black eyes. The previous week she had gone into The Cricketers for a quiet glass of stout when Mrs Willet, Horace's wife, told her to go outside.

When she obeyed, Mrs Willet hit her, knocking her down. While she was on the ground, she said that Horace Willet punched and kicked her. Mrs Willet denied this, saying that her husband had not even been there. Horace agreed, informing the court that his wife and Jane Saunders had had 'a fair fight'. The magistrate bound both parties over to keep the peace.

Sorbo works

On Saturday, 5 June, Lady Henderson laid the foundation stone for the new Sorbo Rubber Products.

War memorials erected

After the war most villages and towns decided to erect memorials in memory of those who had died in defence of their country. In Woking a war memorial committee was formed and £4,000 was raised. It was decided that as part of the town's memorial an extension should be built on to the Woking Victoria Hospital, situated in Chobham Road, near the canal. The sum of £2,000 was donated to the hospital for this purpose and the other £2,000 was to be used for a war memorial.

In July a war memorial was dedicated and unveiled outside St Nicholas Church, Pyrford and later a village hall was also built as a lasting memorial to those who had died. In the same month a memorial was unveiled at All Saints, Woodham. This, unusually, also identified the place where the servicemen had died.

The war memorial at St Peter's, Old Woking, was unveiled and dedicated on 27 November in front of a large crowd. The service, held in the churchyard, was led by the vicar, Reverend Askwith, and wreaths were laid after the address.

Gordon Boys' Home prize-giving

On 11 June, the annual prize-giving was held at the Gordon Boys' Home at West End, Chobham. Princess Mary presented the prizes and she also laid the foundation stone of a new memorial workshop which was to be erected in memory of the 151 Old Boys who had given their lives in the war. This was later to be used as a museum to house all the Gordon memorabilia that the school had collected.

Fire at Martinsydes

Soon after midday on Saturday, 25 September, a fire started at Martinsydes factory. The one thousand employees had just left and only two men remained to finish some work. It was some time before they realised that a fire was raging at the town end of the building beside the railway line. They raised the alarm and Martinsydes' own well-equipped fire service was quickly on the scene followed by Woking fire brigade.

The fire spread rapidly and it was not until about four o'clock that it was finally extinguished. Five workshops had been demolished. The plant was closed for two weeks for repair. Work then proceeded as usual and fortunately there were no job losses.

1921

Musical exercises

On 30 April, the composer, Dr Ethel Smyth, conducted the 'love duet' from her own opera, *The Wreckers*, at the Queen's Hall symphony concert. She felt that a conductor 'must keep the body rigidly under control' and she had an unusual method of training herself to do this.

Neighbours were intrigued to see the composer tie herself to a tree in her garden at Hookheath and wave an imaginary baton. Apparently she sometimes attached herself to a chair in an effort to keep her body still while using her arms. But a tree was taller and therefore of more use for the purpose.

Drought

During June and July there was a prolonged drought; no rain had fallen for about twelve weeks and the tremendous heat caused a number of heath fires. There were so many that the fire brigade was not called out unless houses were in danger; the fires were never completely extinguished and consequently gave birth to yet more. Eventually they could not be left to burn themselves out and the fire brigade was kept busy dousing them to leave blackened heath land.

1922

War memorial

A competition had been held to design Woking's war memorial on which the names of the 550 residents who had given their lives were to be inscribed. The judge was the celebrated architect Sir Edwin Lutyens, who had designed the London Cenotaph. There were forty entries and the winner was Doyle Jones. His design represented 'Victory bringing Peace'. High above the stone column on which the names were written was a life-sized bronze figure; with wings on her shoulders and draped in a cloth, she held aloft the laurel wreath of peace. She became known as 'the Angel of Peace'.

The memorial was erected in Sparrow Park near Victoria Arch. It was covered with a white cloth and draped in a Union Jack. The tassel and cord that would be used for the unveiling had already been used at many other important events. Among those who had pulled this particular cord were Queen Victoria, Edward VII and George V.

The latest to use it was Field Marshal Sir William Robertson who unveiled Woking's war memorial on Empire Day, 24 May. The band was provided by the Queen's Royal Regiment and local church choirs led the singing.

New drama society

This year saw the formation of what is now the oldest drama society in the Woking area – Horsell Amateur Dramatic Society. A number of potential thespians had met above a bank in Horsell and in June 1921 they performed a play called *Our Flat* to an invited audience. It was so successful that they decided to form a drama society.

The society's first public performance was given in Horsell parish hall on 2 February 1922. It was a popular social occasion and the audience wore evening dress. The play was a comedy by Douglas Murray entitled *The Man from Toronto*, and the *Woking News and Mail* described it as 'a distinct triumph'. As a result many would-be actors and actresses applied to join the society but its standards were high and not all were accepted. However, one man who did become a member and took part in five productions was Patrick Moore, who was teaching at St Andrew's preparatory school in Horsell. His photographic memory proved a great asset.

Mobile homes

David Bayliss and his family lived in Lower Robin Hill Road, Knaphill. Their home consisted of four structures described by Mr Bayliss as caravans because they could be moved. Woking Urban District Council disagreed. It said the habitations were 'a disgrace to civilisation' and, as no plans had been submitted, they had no right to be taking up space in Knaphill.

Mr Bayliss was taken to court. He was so determined to prove his point that he drove two of his 'houses' to Woking Police Court to prove they were caravans and could be moved. The council had been told by the sanitary inspector that as the wheels were in the middle of the erections, they would be difficult to move.

When asked by the magistrate how he had managed to get them to court, Mr Bayliss replied cheekily: 'By putting the horses into the shafts and telling them to go.' The bench was not amused and decided that the caravans did constitute a new building and fined Mr Bayliss £2.

Shopping therapy

On 9 November, Woking Chamber of Trade launched Woking and District Shopping Week. Its aim was to make the area better for shopping and to show that Woking could cater for every need. The streets were decorated with bunting, and window dressers produced attractive and unusual displays. There were competitions, displays, demonstrations, recitals and even wireless concerts. The event was greeted with great enthusiasm and crowds thronged the shops.

1923

A lady resigns

Lady Betty Balfour resigned as councillor for St John's. She had held the post for five years and felt honoured to have done so; however, because of other commitments, she was unable to devote as much time to council business as she would like and often had to miss meetings. She therefore felt that she had to resign.

Baby killer

Although Ellen Gregory was twenty, she had the mental age of a 12-year-old. She was employed as a daily domestic servant at the White Hart in Old Woking. Unmarried, she lived with her parents in Send Road, Old Woking.

On 23 March she was unwell and did not go to work. Her mother called the district nurse, who found Ellen lying in bed. She looked very ill and told the nurse that she had had a miscarriage. But when the nurse examined her, she was horrified to discover that the young woman had just given birth, although here was no sign of a baby.

At first Gregory said there was no baby and then she said she had hidden it under the bed. The nurse looked but found nothing. Then she lifted up the mattress and found the newly born child between the mattress and the bed. A coat belt had been tied tightly round its neck. The little body was still warm but there was no sign of life and the nurse could not revive the baby.

Dr Robert Wallace was called and gave the cause of death as asphyxiation due to strangulation. The police became involved and Gregory was arrested on a charge of concealing a birth. At the inquest, the coroner returned an open verdict. Later, however, the girl was charged with murder; the doctor insisted that the birth had been normal and the baby had briefly lived an existence separate from its mother. Ellen Gregory was sent for trial and pleaded not guilty. The judge listened to the evidence and decided that her mind had been unbalanced. He took her mental state into account and sentenced her to twelve months in prison.

Carnival

In June a carnival was held to raise money for the cottage hospital. It was opened in front of the council offices and a traditionally garbed herald announced the coronation of the carnival queen who had been selected by secret ballot. She was to be Mrs Hutchinson Driver. The coronation ceremony was impressive and a speech was read by the queen's 'prime minister'.

A procession of floats then made its way to the cottage hospital, where the carnival queen visited patients. During the following week, there were fetes, plays and competitions, which raised a great deal of money for the hospital.

Girls' Secondary School opens

In September the new Girls' Secondary School opened. Because a new school was desperately needed, it was housed temporarily in four huts that had been used by the army during the first world war. These were linked by covered pathways but the sides were open to the elements. During the winter the girls had to battle against wind, snow and rain in order to go from one classroom to another. Keeping their books in pristine condition must have been difficult! In summer, of course, the girls could dawdle across the 'bridges' soaking up the sun when it appeared.

In spite of the difficulties, good use was made of the huts and they provided temporary housing for an excellent establishment that became the Girls' Grammar School. One of them did triple service as a hall, gymnasium and dining room; every morning the headmistress would face the assembled school from the hall platform.

The first headmistress was Miss Katherine Maris who was chosen from 160 applicants. Educated at Perse High School for Girls in Cambridge, she then went on to obtain a first class degree in science from Newnham College, Cambridge. Presumably she had been introduced to the four army huts that were to be her school before she accepted the post.

1924

Speedy viscount

Viscount Curzon enjoyed speed. Unfortunately when he drove his car at over twenty miles per hour, he was breaking the law. But he had not learnt his lesson. He already had twenty-two convictions for speeding when he was stopped by the police on 30 March on the London road near Ripley. He was travelling at almost twice the speed limit and, when the police charged him, he suggested they should 'make it a bit less' and pleaded with them to 'let me off as lightly as you can'.

When he appeared in court, the magistrate was not impressed with his behaviour. His licence had already been endorsed; this time it was suspended and he was also fined £5.

Crime of passion

Alfred Jones, the proprietor of the Blue Anchor hotel in Byfleet, was a heavy drinker. In the morning he assuaged the inevitable hangover with a dose of Bromo-Seltzer, which was kept in a glass bottle on the mantelpiece in the bar parlour.

His attractive wife, Mabel, turned a blind eye to his drinking and ran a small business separately from her husband. Unfortunately the business was not doing very well; she had become stressed and was advised to take a holiday. She chose Biarritz and it was there that she met a Frenchman, Jean Pierre Vaquier. He operated the wireless equipment in the hotel where she was staying.

In spite of the fact that she spoke no French, and he no English, they were attracted to each other and embarked on an affair. He was infatuated but her feelings were less strong and so she decided to return to Byfleet. She arrived home on 8 February and a week later Vaquier followed her; he arrived, uninvited, at the Blue Anchor knowing that the landlord was away from home. He was penniless and Alfred Jones returned to find a non-paying guest in his hotel. He apparently accepted the situation as his wife had assured him that the affair was over.

However, the Frenchman had not accepted this and was determined to revive it in a most unpleasant way. On 28 March a party was held at the hotel and Alfred Jones, as usual, drank too much. The following morning he staggered down to the bar parlour to mix his Bromo-Seltzer. Having drunk it, he complained that it had an unusually bitter taste. This was not surprising as the medicine had been laced with strychnine. Although Vaquier had been seen washing the bottle after the victim had drunk its contents, traces of the poison remained.

Alfred Jones died in agony in spite of efforts to revive him. Vaquier was charged with his murder and found guilty. He went to the gallows protesting his innocence, although the evidence against him was overwhelming.

The King's speech

On 23 April King George V opened the British Empire Exhibition at Wembley. His speech was broadcast on the wireless and a number of Woking residents were invited to the showroom of Messrs Heath and Wiltshire to hear it; not all enthusiasts owned wirelesses so they were delighted to accept.

It was a very successful demonstration of the use of the wireless. The King's words were heard very clearly and the audience was also able to listen to the massed bands and choir.

Stone-laying ceremony

On 30 April two stones were laid to start an extension to the Percy Street Baptist Church, which had been founded in 1874. There had been an appeal for funds and a substantial sum had already been raised. A number of VIPs watched the stone-laying ceremony, which was performed with beautiful ivory-handled silver-trowels.

The stone on the right-hand side of the entrance was laid by Mr Marnham, the former president of the Baptist Union. As he did so, he said, 'I declare this stone well and truly laid to the glory of God and to the extension of His Kingdom.' The stone on the left side was laid by Mr Serpell, the High Sheriff of Surrey and a member of the Percy Street Baptist Church. He said it was laid 'in the name of the Father, of the Son and of the Holy Ghost'.

The flying vicar

An ex-curate of Christ Church had recently moved to Australia. His parish of Wilcannia covered an area of 40,000 square miles – as big as England. He wrote to the Woking parish appealing for an aeroplane to help him visit his parishioners. By rail or road it took him several days to reach the outlying areas. As he had served in the RAF during the war, he was used to flying. Whether anyone had a spare plane lying unused in the back garden is not known.

1925

The Wreckers

On 10 February, at the Palace Theatre, Woking Musical Society performed its second concert of the season to a full house. One of the pieces performed was the overture to *The Wreckers* composed by Dr Ethel Smyth, who was vice-president of the society and whose music was known all over the world. On this occasion she conducted her own work; the orchestra gave 'an impressive and spirited interpretation' of the overture and it was received enthusiastically by the audience, many of whom considered it the most enjoyable item on the programme.

Capital punishment

On 18 February an interesting meeting of the Women's Citizen's Association was held at the Boys' Secondary School. The speaker, Mrs Matthews of the

Howard League for Penal Reform, gave her views on capital punishment. She considered it should be abolished as she felt it was no deterrent to murder; she suggested that those who carried out the sentence were also guilty of murder and those who advocated it were often motivated only by revenge.

Parking problems

In June three people were summonsed for parking their cars in such a way that they caused an obstruction on the highway. Two offences occurred on 5 June and were the first cases of this kind to be brought before the Woking Petty Sessions.

Gertrude Yates-Smith of the Ridgway, Horsell, parked outside the Bank Chambers in Chertsey Road at about ten o'clock and left her car there for over half an hour. As the road was only wide enough for two cars, the police had to hold up the traffic and operate a one-way system to allow cars to pass both ways. Winifred Kay, who lived in the officers' quarters in Inkerman Barracks, also caused an obstruction by parking outside Knights' premises for some time. The police advised the magistrate that they would not press for a penalty as both were first offences. The cases were dismissed but both women had to pay six shillings in costs.

A few days later Horatio Strachan was also summonsed for the same offence. The bench was told that his parked car had 'caused considerable inconvenience to traffic'. Irritated, Mr Strachan retorted that he had been driving for thirteen years and there was nowhere else to park. He also had to pay the costs.

Hail Caesar

On 8 September a man went into Woking police station and confessed to a number of unsolved murders. When asked his name, he told the policeman he was Julius Caesar VI. Concerned, the officer in charge called the police doctor who examined the man and agreed that his mind was not sound. The self-confessed murderer was charged with being 'a wandering lunatic' and was committed to Brookwood mental hospital.

Mosque visitor

On Friday, 9 October an important visitor joined the local Muslims at prayer in the mosque. She was Her Highness Nawab Sultan Jehan Begum, the ruler of Bhopal, India. Heavily veiled, she wore a jade-green satin-dress and a turban. Her three daughters, who accompanied her, wore brown velour coats and cream hats.

Her visit attracted Muslims from all over Britain as well as other parts of the world. She was greeted by the Imam and, after the prayers, she moved outside where, under an awning, Lord Headley, president of the British Muslim Society, officially welcomed her to Woking. She replied in her own language pausing for her words to be translated into English.

1926

Walker buys Martinsyde's

James Walker took over Martinsyde's factory on the corner of Oriental Road and Maybury Hill. The company had been founded in the 1880s by James Walker, a Scottish engineer who had based his company in London. It made high-pressure seals and gaskets and eventually managed to produce a new packing for use with marine engines. This was marketed under the name of Lion Brand. The company also specialised in the high-pressure seals used by shipbuilders, as well as by car and rail engineers, and James Walker and Lion Brand were inextricably linked.

The business grew and in 1926 the work force of 350 was too large to be accommodated in the London factory so more space was needed and the disused Martinsyde factory was bought. All the manufacturing was moved from London and the Lion Works site was developed.

A tragic death

On 19 February a woman went to draw water from a well near her garden in West End. She received a shock when she saw a pair of feet sticking out of the top. Peering in, she could see they were attached to the body of a woman. Feeling sick, she rushed off to summon the police.

The body of Mrs Florence Gosden was removed from the well and a doctor certified that she was dead and that the cause of death was probably drowning. This was later confirmed. At the inquest Mrs Gosden's husband said that he had last seen his wife on the Wednesday morning before her death. He was a bricklayer and was working in Maidenhead. His wife had visited him on Tuesday and returned home on the Wednesday.

He admitted that she had been worried about a boy who, although he was in their care, had recently been made a ward of court. The couple had also had an argument about some war bonds and Mr Gosden admitted that his wife was probably depressed although he had not noticed it; he had not tried to find out if anything else was troubling her. The coroner ruled that the death could not have been accidental and that Mrs Gosden had taken her own life 'while temporarily insane'.

Shopping week

In April the Woking Chamber of Trade held a British Empire shopping week, which was opened in front of the council buildings by the Earl of Meath. The event was organised in response to a government request to a number of towns. Its object was to improve British trade and to create local employment.

There were various competitions, including one for the best window display. There were also a number of essay competitions for children, all of which related to the Empire. One of them asked, 'Which are the three best Empire shop windows in Woking and district and why?' Two other titles were: 'Why should we buy Empire goods?' and 'Which part of the Empire would you most like to visit? How would you get there and what would you expect to see?' The week was a great success.

The jamboree

At the beginning of June a jamboree was held in the grounds of the Southern Railway Orphanage. It was opened by the founder of the Scout movement, Sir Robert Baden-Powell. 1,000 Scouts, comprising fifteen Scout troops and fourteen Wolf Cub packs, marched past their Chief Scout who was impressed and paid tribute to the achievements of Woking Scouts.

Blackout

On 2 November the whole of Byfleet was plunged into darkness. It was *not* in preparation for 5 November. Just after eight o'clock, the streets went dark, lights in houses and shops disappeared and a black-out in the village hall caused momentary chaos on the dance floor where the local Conservative Party was holding its annual dance.

An investigation revealed that a mouse was the cause of the trouble. The dead animal was discovered underneath the switchboard at the Electric Light Works in Woking. It had been electrocuted when its curiosity led it to squeeze between the bars of the switchboard causing a short circuit; this affected the switch controlling the Byfleet area.

The local authority was presented with the preserved mouse as a contribution to the National Rat Week Campaign!

Baby makes history

In June 1924 Mary Gomme, who had been born in Pollard Road, Woking, had married Reverend Lesley Garrett in Canada, where her family had emigrated. He was a missionary in charge of the Trout Lake Mission in the Severn River district of Canada, the home of the Cree Indians. After the wedding Mary accompanied her husband to the area causing bewilderment among the Indians, who had never seen a white woman before.

Two years later she gave birth to a baby and had to rely on the Indian women for help as the nearest white people were over a hundred miles away. The Indians were fascinated by the new arrival. They sat in a circle round the tiny creature admiring it. Mary was no longer known as the 'missionary's wife'. She was elevated to the status of the 'baby's mother'!

1927

Silence is golden

Motorcycles were no longer a male prerogative and a race for women was organised by Wood Green motor club. On 14 January, Miss A. G. M. Broderick of Woking won a special prize in this race. It was for the most silent machine.

Plaza opens

In February the new Plaza cinema in Chertsey Road was opened by the chairman of the district council in front of a large audience that included a number of public figures. It was on the site of the old Central cinema, which had been completely redesigned. Described as one of the best cinemas outside London, the doors opened on to a large entrance hall. On either side carpeted staircases led up to a spacious balcony. The luxurious seating and attractive colour scheme were highlighted by the unusual lighting effects, which glided through varying shades of orange, red and blue.

After the singing of the national anthem, the curtain went up. The first film to be shown in the new building was *Mons*, a fitting memorial to those who had given their lives in the Great War. It was followed by a short comedy and a musical interlude from an orchestra.

Following the opening of the new cinema, there was a huge demand for tickets. Those on the ground floor were priced at sixpence, nine pence, one shilling and one shilling and three pence. Balcony seats, which could be booked, cost one shilling and sixpence. There was one performance each evening apart from Saturday, on which there were two. As an added attraction there was a musical interlude each evening.

An enterprising lady

Mrs Sybil Methold was an enterprising lady who had no intention of sitting at home doing nothing. Watching more and more cars appear on the roads, she realised that a well-run service-station would be an excellent business proposition.

She found a suitable site in a field covered with redcurrant bushes, at one end of which was a large oak tree. She was determined that the service station would blend in with the countryside and to this end, having disposed of the redcurrant bushes, she designed and built it around the oak tree. At that time all petrol companies devised their own distinctive colour schemes and Mrs Methold was no exception.

She was adamant that her eight petrol pumps should all be the same colour. Having an eye for detail, she noticed that there was a streak of pale green lichen on the trunk of the oak tree and she decided to use that colour for the pumps. She faced great opposition from other petrol companies but was not deterred. Eventually she persuaded them to accept her colour scheme and she had the paint blended specially for her by Parson's Paints of Mitcham. When the painting was completed, she added more colour by planting a multitude of bulbs in the forecourt. She did not forget that some motorists might be travelling at night and installed a shilling-in-the-slot machine for their convenience, while a motor-repair shop took care of any mechanical problems.

The Mid-Surrey service station opened at Easter and the enterprise was so successful that Mrs Methold's husband, Montague, soon gave up his own business in Guildford to join her. He eventually became one of the first fellows of the Institute of the Motor Trade. The Metholds provided personal service and before long their name appeared not only in the local press but also in the national papers. Motorists sang their praises and were particularly appreciative of services rendered to them in the middle of the night.

An unusual amputation

On 5 February a Mrs Hockley stepped off a bus in Brox Road, Ottershaw. Unfortunately, the bus moved off before she could get out of the way and it ran her over, badly damaging her left leg. There was no time to take her to hospital and her leg had to be amputated in the street. She showed great fortitude during the operation and did not lose consciousness. She was eventually taken to Ottershaw infirmary.

Unfortunate accident

Stephen Perks of Knaphill was only two months' old when he died. It was an unnecessary death brought about by poverty. His mother, father and two other children slept in the same bed while another child was in a cot in the same room. Apparently there was no space for another cot.

At the inquest into the child's death, his mother explained what had happened. She said that she had joined her two children in the bed at half past ten; her husband, a bus driver, had climbed into the same bed about two hours later. During the night Stephen had become restless and she had turned over to feed him. She was tired and went straight back to sleep not noticing that he had rolled towards the other child. In the morning when she woke up, she realised that her youngest son had suffocated under his sibling's body. Having woken her husband, she sent for the district nurse who, sure that the child was dead, immediately called the doctor; he certified that Stephen had died from asphyxiation. The coroner was disturbed that the children slept in the same bed as their parents and felt that anything was better than that.

'Perhaps a drawer in a chest of drawers,' he suggested kindly. 'I have no chest of drawers, sir,' replied Mrs Perks sadly.

The coroner decided that both parents had done their best under very difficult circumstances and returned a verdict of accidental death.

1928

Floods

The year started with the worst floods in living memory. There had been a heavy snowfall and, when the snow thawed, the rain started. The low-lying areas of Chobham, Horsell and Old Woking suffered the most. Chobham village was completely cut off from its surroundings and Unwin Printing Works in Old Woking had to be shut down. At Elmbridge near the Woking sports ground, part of the road was under a foot of water and the fields around it resembled a lake.

Once again the residents of Old Woking were trapped inside their houses. One enterprising gentleman carried two chairs with him to help him travel from his house to dry land. He had quite a distance to go. The river-like appearance of High Street in Old Woking attracted a family of swans. The graceful creatures with their brood of cygnets swam up and down graciously accepting the offerings of bread thrown to them by the marooned residents from their upstairs windows.

The water rose to a depth of over two feet before finally subsiding. The rainfall was the heaviest ever recorded in the Woking area.

Library opens

The old Roman Catholic chapel in Percy Street had been converted into Woking's first public library. It was officially opened on 18 January by Lieutenant-Colonel Matthews, chairman of Woking Urban District Council. To join the library, Woking residents could fill in a form, which had to be countersigned by a ratepayer. Books could be kept for a fortnight and the fine for overdue books was one penny per week or part of a week. Within the first month there were more than a thousand borrowers and the number was steadily rising.

A prize for Sybil

Mrs Sybil Methold won third prize out of 14,000 entrants in a ministry of transport competition for her design and decoration of the Mid-Surrey service station in Ripley. She should perhaps have been awarded the first prize as apparently the designs of the first and second winners were still at the planning stage and were never built.

Woking Music Festival

At the end of November the first Woking musical festival was held at the Woking Boys' Secondary School. It was a great success. There were 1,500 entries in the forty competitions, in which both adults and children took part. There were classes for vocal and instrumental solos, choirs and orchestras. First prizes in their particular competitions were won by the choirs of Woking County School Old Girls' Association and Woking Congregational Church. The judges were very impressed by the high standard of all the performers and it was hoped that the festival would become an annual event.

Nothing like a Dame

Another musical event took place at the beginning of December, also at the Boys' Secondary School. This was the first concert of the Woking Musical Society's thirty-first season and it was to celebrate the golden jubilee of Dame Ethel Smyth – the greatest living woman composer – who lived in Woking and was vice-president of the society. It was fifty years before that her first composition had been performed in public.

The concert consisted mainly of works by Dame Edith and she, herself, conducted them to enthusiastic applause from the audience. There were songs and madrigals and one of the most popular pieces of the first part of the evening was the overture to her opera *The Boatswain's Mate*.

During the interval a cheque was presented to the composer to commemorate her jubilee. The collection had been organised by Lady Betty Balfour who, unfortunately, was unable to be present. The following week a celebration concert was to be held in Berlin and Dame Edith referred to this in her acceptance speech.

She said, 'I do really think that this affair in Germany will have a great repercussion upon the thing I care more about than anything else – the position of women in music. I shall have the very great honour of being the first woman who has ever conducted the Berlin Philharmonic Orchestra.'

After the interval, at her request, the orchestra, choir and audience joined in her famous *The March of the Women*, which had been composed to support the suffragette movement. Dame Edith conducted it. She told the audience that in future it would be known as *The March of the People* as the suffragettes had eventually won their battle. She intended to write some new words to it while she was travelling to Germany.

1929

Prizes for Horsell

Horsell Church of England School covered itself in glory in March. The school took part in the West Surrey branch of the English Folk Dance Society competition held in Guildford. The under-eighteen mixed team and the under-ten team both carried off the first prizes in their particular classes while the Horsell Boys' team were second. Goldsworth Junior School under-ten team came second.

Attempted murder

Annie Chapman (43) separated from her husband in July 1928. She was not pleased when he went to lodge next door with her widowed sister, Harriet Brown. Both cottages in Ripley were detached and there was only about 150 yards between them. Because of this there was tension between the two sisters, who rarely spoke, but the anger and jealousy felt by Annie continued to fester.

In the scullery of Brown's house a double-barrelled shotgun was kept. Her sister knew this and, on 22 April, she stole it. Then she sat down to write hysterical letters to her husband, daughter, the police and the coroner. She told the latter that she was 'not insane'.

The following day, Harriet Brown was in her garden when she felt something whizz past her ear. Looking round she saw her sister pointing a gun at her through the bushes. As she ran into her neighbour's house, there was another shot but it missed her. She and the neighbour rushed into the house slamming the door while Annie hammered on it trying to force an entry. Failing to do this, she next smashed a window, opened it and fired into the kitchen, where the two women were standing. Fortunately the bullet missed them and hit a sack before embedding itself in the floor.

At that moment Sydney Heard, a dairyman, passed by. Realising what was happening, he grabbed the hysterical woman and wrestled the gun from her. When Harriet came out, Annie attacked her, tearing her blouse, shouting that her sister had stolen her husband and threatening to 'do her in'. By the time the police arrived, she had calmed down a little but told them, 'Take me to the police station. I intended to do her in and then do myself in.'

At her trial at the Old Bailey she pleaded not guilty to the charges of attempted murder and of attempting to cause grievous bodily harm. She told the judge she had only intended to frighten her sister because she was upset about her husband's friendship with her. The jury of eight men and four women took just fifteen minutes to find her guilty of attempting to cause grievous bodily harm but innocent of attempted murder. They also added a plea for mercy. The judge took note of this and bound Annie over for two years.

1930

Hooray for Henry

At the end of December 1929, Henry Howard retired from Woking post office after serving it for over forty years. He had started working there in 1889. During that time he had regularly delivered the post either on foot or on his bicycle.

On 22 April 1930 at the Woking sorting ofice in White Rose Lane he was presented with the Imperial Services Medal for long, faithful and zealous service. The presentation was made by Mr Woodward, the Woking post office assistant-superintendent. Unfortunately Major Black, the postmaster, was unable to be present. The medal, awarded by the King, was engraved on one side with the words 'for Faithful Service' and on the other side was the King's head. Mr Howard's name was inscribed on the rim.

Crash at Brooklands

In May a very unpleasant accident occurred at Brooklands. Two Talbot cars, competing in the Double Twelve Hours race, were travelling at eighty-five miles per hour when they collided. The force of the collision caused them to swerve off the track and crash through the railings into the crowd of spectators. Two men were killed and twelve other spectators were seriously injured. It was late into the evening before the ambulances finished ferrying the injured to hospital.

One of the dead men was a Mr Harworth. It was his first visit to Brooklands and, sadly, it was to be his last. The other victim was Edward Ellery, a mechanic who was a passenger in one of the cars. It was the first time he had taken part in a race although he had been a mechanic for seven years.

At the inquest the jury brought in a verdict of accidental death on the mechanic and 'death from misadventure' on the spectator. The jury also strongly recommended that there should be stricter supervision at motor races.

Coat of arms

On the last Saturday of September an important event took place at the council offices. The High Sheriff of Surrey, Mr Serpel, gave a banquet for Woking dignitaries. Afterwards he presented Mr Quartermaine, chairman of the council, with a document that authorised the use of a coat of arms for the town. The arms were based in the history of Woking and incorporated symbols from the coats of arms of families who had been connected with the town, including the Beauforts. The motto at the bottom read *Fide et Diligentia* (faithful and diligent).

Mr Quartermaine was also invested with a blue silk robe trimmed with velvet and ermine. Round his neck was hung a gold chain of office, which was to be worn by successive chairmen. It consisted of twenty-six solid gold shields on each of which was engraved the names of three chairmen of the council. The first name was that of Mr Wernig who had been appointed the first chairman in 1895.

Chairman's chair

In October, Mr Whitburn, the oldest member of Woking Council, presented a chair for the use of council chairmen. Mr Whitburn had first been elected to office in 1905 and had been chairman in 1913–14. The chair was made of oak and upholstered in red Moroccan leather. The top of the chair contained the coat of arms and underneath this there was a gilt metal tablet which read: 'This chair was presented October 1930 to the Urban District Council of Woking by Councillor Henry Whitburn to commemorate his 26 consecutive years of office.'

At each side of the chair the curved arms were supported by pillars. On the feet of the massive legs were castors for ease of moving and there were also handles so that the chair could be carried if necessary.

1931

It's fun to stay at . . .

In March new YMCA premises in Bath Road were opened. The centre was created for young men of sixteen and over who were encouraged to 'make it (their) home for leisure hours and to say goodbye to lonely evenings'. It was to open every weekday from ten in the morning until ten in the evening.

The work had been funded by businessmen and residents of Woking but £600 was still needed to meet the cost of the building, which contained a spacious lounge, a hall with a stage, a billiard room and a games room.

Monster in Woking

On Saturday 1 August a prehistoric monster was paraded through the streets of Woking by 'strangely dressed keepers' who sold flags to passers-by. 'Walter' had been created by the YMCA to raise some much-needed funds. He had been dragged out of his 'den' at the YMCA in Bath Road for the purpose. About forty feet long, it had taken about a month to make him out of canvas, which was then painted. A notice on his back stated that he would later be returned to Whipsnade Zoo.

The council had, very unkindly, refused him entrance to the recreation ground and for long periods of time he was 'parked' outside the Grand Hotel while his 'keepers' wound up a barrel organ to entertain the crowds and raise more money. About £50 was raised during the day.

1932

Slimming tragedy

Miss Evelyn Rouse was of a cheerful and placid disposition. She was thirty-one years old and lived with her mother, sister and two maids in West Byfleet. She kept herself very busy with voluntary work and was a well-known local tennis player.

But one thing worried her. She knew she was too fat and was determined to lose weight. She had recently lost a stone but she did not consider that sufficient and was always trying out new methods of slimming. One of these was a special form of massage.

Sadly this went very wrong. One evening at the end of January, she went to her bedroom to prepare for bed. But she did not go to bed. Putting on her dressing gown, she went to a drawer and extracted a long scarf from it. Tying each end to the bed post at the end of her bed, she sat on the floor slipping her head into the 'noose' she had made. As instructed, she carried out the exercise gently rubbing her neck back and forth on the scarf.

When her maid went to call her early the next morning, she found her mistress dead on the floor. Her scarf had wound itself round her neck strangling her. At the inquest, the coroner brought in a verdict of 'death from misadventure'. He assumed she had been massaging her neck with the scarf in an effort to slim; he pointed out that this was an extremely dangerous practice and other young women, who were addicted to slimming, should beware of it.

St Mary's tower

When work started on the restoration of the church tower of St Mary's, Horsell, there was a startling development. The tower had been restored a few years previously but it had not been done well. When the outer casing of the botched restoration was removed the restorers discovered the original stone tower, which had been built about 1340. It was then decided to restore the tower as far as was possible to its original glory. It had originally contained three clock-faces but the one over the main doorway had to be removed.

Head retires

At the end of July the Boys' Secondary School held its eighteenth annual speech day. It was a moving occasion as Mr Holden, the headmaster, was retiring after having been at the school since it opened. He had watched the school grow from small beginnings and the current number of boys on the roll was 331; boys from the school had made their mark all over the world. Mr Holden was presented with a set of the *Encyclopaedia Britannica* and the proceedings closed with three cheers for the retiring headmaster followed by the national anthem. The new head was a Mr Huggins from St Albans.

Guide celebration

The Girl Guide movement started in 1911 and in June its twenty-first birthday was celebrated throughout the world. Woking held a week of celebrations. One thousand Girl Guides from Woking and surrounding districts paraded through the streets to Wheatsheaf Common where a large crowd watched the district commissioner, Miss Warren, take the salute. The Guides then marched to Christ Church for a special thanksgiving service conducted by the vicar, Reverend Clifford, who was assisted by Reverend Johnson representing the Free Churches.

Then the Guides returned to Wheatsheaf Common for the closing ceremony of the week; they heard Miss Warren read out a message from the Chief Guide, Lady Baden-Powell.

1933

Eightieth birthday

On Sunday, 30 April Mr Serpel, the former High Sheriff of Surrey and the current Deputy Lieutenant of the county, celebrated his eightieth birthday. In the morning he attended the service at Woking Baptist Church where he was a member. For the rest of the day he entertained members of his family who visited him to give their congratulations and best wishes. Despite his age, he still travelled to London on business nearly every day.

Out of Africa

At the end of August the church of St Mary of Bethany in Mount Hermon Road had a visitor from Nigeria. He was Bishop Akinyele, principal of the grammar school in Ibadan in the Lagos diocese. He thanked the Woking parishes for their 'generous support' given to the 'mission fields'.

Fires

Because of the dry summer, there were several outbreaks of fire in Horsell in September and the air was filled with the scent of burnt pine wood. The fire brigade was kept very busy but passers-by also stopped to help by beating out the flames with large branches from the trees. Firemen were on duty at Horsell Common for six or seven hours at a time and, when the fires were finally extinguished, a huge blackened waste was left as a reminder. There were also fires in Horsell Birch and White Rose Lane but fortunately no houses were damaged.

Balloons go up

On the afternoon of 13 September the YMCA released some balloons from the garden of Ashwood House in Woking. The following morning one was found near Schelswig in North Germany. A German paper reported this and a cutting with the following translation was sent to Woking:

> A balloon was found by a farmer near here. Attached to it was a piece of

paper saying that the balloon was released in Woking on 13 September. The balloon was 'found' on 14 September. The 'founder' has been promised a reward of five shillings.

A number of balloons were returned from all over England and from Holland and Belgium as well as Germany. One from a young German had a note attached: 'I would request you to write a letter to me. I should like to have a letter from an Englishman.'

Old Contemptibles

In October the Old Contemptibles Association paraded 300 men at a special service in Christ Church. The occasion was the dedication of a new standard and fourteen branches of the association joined the Woking branch to celebrate this. Many of the men had been maimed in the war and after the service they marched through the town to the war memorial in Sparrow Park.

Bonfire

The Ripley and Ockham Bonfire Boys' Association built a huge bonfire on Ripley Green for Guy Fawkes night. It was forty-feet high and the diameter at the base was thirty-five feet. On Saturday 4 November the boys marched from Ockham to Ripley and lit the bonfire to start the celebrations for bonfire night. A spectacular firework display followed.

1934

Open for business

William Robinson opened his first shop in Chertsey Road. He had moved from Leicester to Woking and had bought Alfred Wyles's drapers shop in Chertsey Road. Robinson's was a family business, which aimed to provide excellent service and good quality. The firm was later run by his son, David, and his daughter Isabel.

The shop soon became very popular as a drapery store and ladies' outfitters. Chauffeur-driven cars would occasionally park outside the shop and, while the drivers went for a walk, the sales assistants would get into the car to measure the elderly lady occupants for their corsets!

The restaurant on the upper floor was the only one in Chertsey Road and the catering firm was the same as the one used by Harrods of Knightsbridge.

That darned cat

On the evening of Saturday, 5 May a large black-and-white cat climbed to the top of the seventy-five-foot water-cooling tower at the Woking Electric Company. It was probably chasing some elusive pigeons but, having reached the top, it found it impossible to climb down again.

The fire brigade was called and worked until dark with ladders and fire escapes to rescue it. But every time they approached, the cat dodged away from them. Although it could not get down itself, it did not seem to appreciate help. When it became dark, the firemen felt it was too dangerous to continue so abandoned the rescue attempt for the night.

Early on Sunday morning they changed their tactics and brought fire hoses instead. Knowing how much cats hate water, they played jets of it near the animal, which reacted as expected. In order to avoid the water, it leapt about thirty feet on to a sloping roof. Two more spectacular jumps brought it to the ground to the cheers of the crowd of spectators who had gathered to watch the display. Bewildered by the attention it was receiving, the cat then hurtled over a high fence and disappeared into the distance. The show was over.

Suicide pact

A passer-by made a gruesome discovery early one Thursday morning in July. On his way to work he discovered two dead bodies – a male and a female – on the railway line between Brookwood and Woking. Both were badly mutilated where a train had crushed them but there was an unusual feature. The right hand of the man and the left hand of the girl had been joined together with a handkerchief.

The couple were later identified as Reginald Collyer (31), of Mayford, and his girlfriend, Winifred Colclough, who was twenty. She was a domestic servant and three months' pregnant; they were to be married in August. Winifred's father was very upset by his daughter's death and suggested that Collyer had dragged her to her death. However, there was no sign of a struggle and it seemed more likely that the couple had chosen to link hands before going to their deaths.

At the inquest the jury decided that a suicide pact had been forged although there appeared to be no reason for it. It was decided that the couple were 'temporarily of unsound mind' when they planned their horrific deaths.

Open-air cremation

In July, Chamshere Jung – a Nepalese princess, who had lived in St John's village for some time – died. Because she was a Hindu, the Home Office granted

Woking a licence to hold an open-air cremation; it was the only crematorium ever to have held this licence. The princess was cremated in the grounds of the crematorium in accordance with Hindu religious rites.

House on fire

The year ended with one of the worst fires that there had even been in the Woking area. In the early hours of the last Friday of the year fire broke out at Calluna, a large house in White Rose Lane owned by Mr and Mrs Lancaster. Miss Hill – a nurse, who was sleeping on the top floor of the house – was woken by the smell of smoke about two o'clock in the morning. Going down to the next floor, she discovered that the sitting room beneath her bedroom was ablaze. She hurriedly roused the other occupants of the house. Still wearing their night clothes, Mr and Mrs Lancaster, their son and two maids were able to escape by the front door; the fire escapes that Mr Lancaster had installed were not needed. Fortunately there were no casualties although the house was almost completely destroyed. The cost of repair was later estimated at £5,000.

The fire brigade responded promptly to the call and were at the scene within a quarter of an hour. But there was little they could do to save the house, which was burning furiously. It was difficult to use the hoses on the upstairs rooms as the windows refused to open and consequently the contents of the upper floors were destroyed but most of the furniture from downstairs was saved, including a grand piano. The kitchen was badly damaged by the fire and the other rooms on the lower floors were flooded with water from the hoses and Christmas cards were seen floating amid the debris.

It took four hours to subdue the flames and the remains of the building were still smouldering the following day. It was not known how the fire had started.

1935

Silver jubilee

In May, with the rest of the country, Woking celebrated the silver jubilee of King George V's coronation in style. The estimated cost of the three-day celebration was £900. As usual the streets were decorated with bunting and flags and, on the Saturday afternoon, 273 elderly men and women were entertained to tea in the Grand hotel. The oldest man was Mr Steer of Arnold Road who was ninety-three. The oldest lady was a year younger; she was Mrs Jolly who lived in the High Street, Old Woking. After tea the old folks were entertained by a concert party.

On Sunday afternoon a procession headed by the Salvation Army band and consisting of the British Legion and other local groups, including Scouts and Guides, made its way along Chobham Road to Wheatsheaf Common. Here, an open-air service was held; it was led by Clifford Bonham, vicar of Christ Church, who paid tribute to the King and Queen. In the evening, trees were planted simultaneously at Woking recreation ground, West Byfleet and Knaphill. A concert followed the planting in the recreation ground.

On Monday it was the turn of the children. A tea party was held for 4,000 of them in the recreation ground after some sports activities. Each child was presented with a Jubilee mug. In the evening a crowd of 10,000 listened to the King's radio message to the Empire. The celebrations ended with a firework display.

Taking the plunge

On 5 June two thousand visitors watched the Duke of Sutherland from Sutton Place open Woking's new open-air swimming-pool. It had cost £321,600 but residents agreed that it was money well spent. The pool and its surroundings covered five acres. Grass lanes beside the pool enabled sun worshippers to sunbathe and a café at the eastern end provided drinks and refreshments.

It had rained during the morning of the opening but fortunately it stopped in time for the ceremony, after which there was a display of swimming and diving. One of the main attractions was a Mr Temme, who was the only person to have swum the English Channel in both directions. At quarter past six the pool was open for use by the public. Adults were charged six pence and children three pence.

New Methodist church

At the beginning of November the new Methodist church was opened in Knaphill. It was built on the site of the original 1866 building, which had become too small for the congregation. The new building had been mainly paid for by Mr and Mrs Frank Derry, members of the church for thirty-five years.

A large crowd watched the architect, Mr Kenneth Wood, present Mr Derry with the key to the church. He opened the door and the congregation filed in for the dedication service led by Reverend Ernest Bailey, superintendent of the Woking Circuit.

1936

Death of the King

In the early hours of Tuesday, 21 January King George V died. In Woking the news was first heard by residents who owned wireless sets but it spread quickly through the town and flags were lowered to half mast. Many functions that were due to take place over the next few days were cancelled as a mark of respect.

The following message was sent to the new King, Edward VIII, at St James' Palace by Major Tuckett, president of the Woking branch of the British Legion:

> Members of the Woking Branch, British Legion, deeply mourn the loss of our beloved King and convey to you, Her Majesty, Queen Mary, and all members of the Royal Family, our deepest sympathy in your great bereavement.

A reply came from Buckingham Palace:

> The King is touched by your kind message of sympathy and will be glad if you will express his sincere thanks to all who joined in.

The proclamation of the new King did not take place in Woking as it was not a municipal borough. The funeral was on the following Tuesday, 28 January, and on that day all businesses and shops in Woking were closed. The service was broadcast over the wireless and many people were able to listen. One of the bearers of the King's coffin was Lance-Corporal Holehouse from Knaphill. He had been in the Grenadier Guards for seventeen months and, at six feet six-and-a-half inches, he was the tallest guardsman in the army.

In the afternoon a memorial service was held in Christ Church and representatives from most of the local churches attended. It was led by the vicar, Clifford Banham, and, because the congregation could not all be seated, another service was held simultaneously in Trinity Methodist church. Later, other churches in the area also held memorial services.

The hero of Arthur's Bridge

On a cold day at the end of February a boy from Horsell fell into the Basingstoke canal near Arthur's Bridge. He could not swim and was in danger of drowning when two other boys passed by. William Hammond immediately took off his jacket and plunged into the water fully clothed. His friend, Frank Hack, joined him and together they managed to drag the boy towards the bank and haul him out of the water.

The two boys were later honoured for what they had done. They were pupils at Goldsworth School and in May the whole school watched as Lieutenant-Colonel Easton from the Royal Humane Society presented them with an award for bravery. He told the assembled school that he hoped they would follow their fellow pupils' example and learn to swim. Mr Farr, the headmaster, reminded the school that the new pool had been built with young people in mind and classes for non-swimmers would soon take place there.

Forced landing

Slocock's nurseries in Goldsworth Road had an unexpected visitor one Sunday afternoon in March. A British Klemm monoplane made a forced landing in the middle of a bed of roses. The plane was piloted by Captain Lambert, who was attempting to fly solo from Bristol to Heston.

Unfortunately his engine cut out when he was nearing Woking and residents watched in horror as his plane hurtled earthwards towards a row of houses. Luckily, the pilot managed to steer it over the tops of the buildings and also clear a large oak tree in Goldsworth Road; he then thudded into the nursery and skidded along the ground before coming to rest the right way up in the middle of the rose bushes.

Apparently unharmed, he then nonchalantly climbed out of his badly damaged machine and ambled to a nearby house to telephone for help. By the time he returned, the plane had attracted a number of sightseers. Captain Lambert apologised for the disturbance but told them the nursery was the only safe place he could see to land. The plane was dismantled and removed the following day and only the damaged roses were left as a reminder.

Bees stop play

On the afternoon of Saturday, 16 May, St John's cricket club was playing the Lion Works. Suddenly the players heard a droning noise above them; it seemed to be drawing closer. Looking up, they saw a swarm of bees flying only few feet above the ground. The players dived on to their faces and lay flat while thousands of the insects swarmed over them, crossing the pitch between the wickets. They then soared up and flew over the tower of the nearby church and disappeared into the distance.

Play was resumed after 'bees stopped play'.

Haile Selassie visits Woking

At the end of August a very important gentleman visited Woking. This was Haile Selassie, Emperor of Ethiopia. Wearing a long black cloak, he travelled by car from London and arrived at Woking Mosque about a quarter past three. Here, he was greeted with a bouquet by Madam Buchanan-Hamilton of the British Muslim Society.

Her husband, Sir Abdulla Archibald Hamilton, then welcomed the visitor on behalf of the Muslim community, who, he said, respected the Emperor's faith in God and his tolerance of religions other than his own. This was demonstrated by his visit to the mosque. The Emperor's reply in Arabic was translated and the assembled company then entered the mosque. After a short prayer, the visitor was presented with a copy of the Koran and a book about the Prophet Muhammad.

1937

Putting on the Ritz

On Monday evening, 12 April, the Ritz cinema in Chobham Road opened its doors for the first time. It was described as 'one of the finest cinemas in the United Kingdom . . . the last word in luxury and comfort and a house of entertainment second to none'. It had been built by Union Cinemas Ltd.

The double line of glass doors opened into a spacious foyer with piled carpets and a moulded ceiling. The building was carpeted throughout and the colours were in graded tones of terracotta, peach and gold. The semi-tub seats in the cinema were comfortable and provided ample leg room for tall people.

A magnificent Compton organ had been built specifically for the Ritz and it was installed at great expense. The latest projection technology had been used and air conditioning and central heating guaranteed comfort. A restaurant above the cinema provided an added attraction and, during matinee performances, afternoon tea could be brought to the audience in their seats.

A crowd of 1,600 watched Mr Godfrey Nicholson, MP for Farnham, perform the opening ceremony and the stage show that followed contained a galaxy of well-known stars. Others, including Jack Buchanan and Anna Neagle, sent messages of congratulation. At the organ was Harold Ramsay, the radio organist known all over the world. After the entertainment, which lasted three hours, he led some community singing.

The first film shown was *The Texas Rangers* followed by the comedy, *Wives Never Know*. In future the cinema would be open from ten in the morning to half past ten at night and food would be served in the restaurant all day.

The coronation

After King Edward VIII abdicated, his brother, the Duke of York was proclaimed King George VI. He had a special link with Woking as he was chairman of the executive committee of the Gordon Boys' Home. Every year he attended the annual prize-giving to present the prizes although he had not done so in 1936 because of the death of his father.

His coronation was on 12 May 1937 and, with the rest of the country and the Empire, Woking celebrated. On behalf of Woking Council, the fire brigade had decorated the streets. Unfortunately it poured with rain in the morning but this did not dampen the high spirits of the crowd although some events in Woking had to be cancelled because of the weather.

The Rotary Club organised an old folks' tea in the Grand Hotel while 3,000 children were entertained in the recreation ground. A fancy-dress parade was held and the children were presented with coronation mugs. In Old Woking there was a children's street party where each child was given a cup and saucer filled with sweets by the oldest resident, Mrs Fillingham. Winifred Gunner, aged three, presented her with a bouquet.

At eight o'clock in the evening, following a broadcast of the 'Empire's homage', the new King broadcast a message to his subjects.

Fairoaks opened

In October 1937 Fairoaks airfield at Chobham opened. It was built as part of the expansion of the RAF and housed a Reserve flying-training-school, which had a number of Tiger Moth planes.

1938

Church fire

On Sunday, 9 January the caretaker, as usual, stoked the fire in the church hall of All Saints, Woodham, and arranged the furniture ready for the afternoon Sunday School. He left soon after one o'clock and, about half an hour later, a bus driver, some distance away, saw smoke, which he traced to the burning church hall. He stopped his bus at the vicarage and the vicar, Reverend Samson, hurriedly phoned the fire brigade, which arrived promptly; however they could not save the wooden building or its contents.

When the teachers and their pupils arrived, the hall was a blazing ruin and the staging, crockery, furniture and piano had all, literally, 'gone up in smoke'. The hall was thirty years' old and the burnt-out entrance porch was all that remained. It was a great loss to the parish as the building had been the centre of its social life. At least £1,000 would be needed to replace it.

The Bedser twins

The six-foot, 19-year-old Bedser twins, Alec and Eric, were selected to play professional cricket for Surrey. The promising all-rounders had already played for the Young Players of Surrey and had been members of Woking Cricket Club since they were fourteen. After leaving school, they had worked in a London solicitor's office but their future career would be in the game they loved.

Preparing for war

As war became more likely, Woking's air raid precautions were implemented. By the end of September 1,400 had volunteered but not many of those would be called up if war did break out. Men and women from all walks of life were needed to drive lorries and ambulances, work in offices, give first aid and help in rescue and demolition work.

Arrangements had been made for the evacuation of 1,700 London school children to Woking. They were to be billeted in the schools – which would be closed – until homes could be found for them. However the proposed evacuation was cancelled by the Home Office.

A total of 36,750 gas masks had been dispatched to Woking for delivery to residents by ARP wardens. These had to be assembled and seventy girls were employed for this task but more gas masks were needed. Volunteers were already being trained in decontamination.

The Home Office issued guidelines for households. Each member must learn to use a gas mask and a refuge room should be prepared where cover could be taken if necessary. This could also be used to store essential equipment. It was suggested that, if possible, a trench should be dug in the garden but the nearest public air raid shelter should also be identified.

A speech by the Prime Minister, Neville Chamberlain, was heard by large audiences in the Astoria, Plaza and Ritz cinemas.

1939

New church hall

In January, twelve months after it had been completely destroyed by fire, a new church hall was opened in Woodham. A large audience watched Bishop Golding-Bird perform the opening ceremony. The hall had been erected on the site of the old building but, at £2,600, it had cost twice as much as estimated.

However, the parishioners considered it a worthwhile investment and the new hall was, without doubt, an improvement on the old one. Firstly, it was made of brick not wood! The spacious tiled hall was fitted with a stage at one end and a gallery. There were dressing rooms, a committee room and a fitted kitchen, while the modern heating and lighting systems that had been installed were considerably safer than the boiler that had heated the old hall.

Air-raid shelters

On 10 March the *Woking News and Mail* carried the following advertisement:

> AIR RAID SHELTERS
> Designs and prices of the latest air raid shelter with or without air-conditioning apparatus. Send your enquiries to Messrs ALFRED HARDY & CO. LTD. Kingsway Avenue, WOKING

Cathedral week

The first week in July was designated Guildford Cathedral week in Woking. It was inaugurated on 2 July by the Bishop of Guildford, who preached in Christ Church at the morning service. Woking deanery hoped to raise £5,000 towards the cost of the new cathedral. It was hoped that part of it might be opened in 1941.

The local cinemas all carried a film of the cathedral, showing how the finished building would appear. There were simulated views of both the interior and exterior. The Provost of Guildford, the Very Reverend Eric Southam, was the commentator and the film was shown throughout the week. A paper model of the completed cathedral was displayed in the window of Coleman's store in High Street. Three and a half feet-long, and eighteen inches wide, it had taken Mr Page Grubb of the Hockering Estate four months to make; he had used reinforced paper and coloured it with transparent paint.

On 15 July a United Service of offering and thanksgiving was held. During the morning of the same day Woking residents were able to contribute towards the cost of the cathedral. From ten in the morning until seven at night, the Provost of Guildford sat outside the Albion Hotel, opposite the station, to receive the monetary offerings.

Evacuees

The evacuation of several thousand London children to Woking – which had been postponed in 1938 – finally took place in September 1939. The first group arrived by train about half past nine on the morning of 1 September and others came at intervals throughout the day. It was described as 'a precautionary measure' and the children were met by the billeting officer from the Women's Voluntary Service, which was arranging homes for the children. The evacuees comprised mothers and toddlers as well as teachers with their charges. Many of the children had never left London before, and were bewildered by the countryside surrounding Woking, but they were made very welcome by their hosts and the billeting arrangements went smoothly.

'At war with Germany'

On Sunday, 3 September Woking residents who owned wireless sets heard the Prime Minister's solemn announcement that England was now 'at war with Germany'. Churches later broadcast the news and prayers were said for a speedy end to the conflict.

The ARP services were mobilised and in October the first local casualties of the war were reported in the newspaper. Six men from Woking and the surrounding area had died on HMS *Royal Oak* when she was attacked by a German submarine at Scapa Flow.

In December an air-raid-practice test was held in Woking on a Saturday afternoon. Eight areas were designated as sites of 'bombing' and over two hundred ARP wardens took part, attending to the 'injured', ferrying them to hospital and clearing the 'damage'. An 'enemy plane' was reported as having landed near the Plough Inn in Horsell and the 'pilot' was taken prisoner. The practice was carried out very efficiently and Woking felt that it was prepared for any emergency.

'Sittings' in Christ Church

For many years it had been the custom for church pews to be 'reserved' for particular families or individuals. A seat could be reserved for the price of a guinea (twenty-one shillings). This was a divisive practice as those who could afford to pay were guaranteed the seat of their choice while the rest had to sit where they could.

Christ Church was no exception and enjoyed the extra revenue that reserved seats provided. The custom was not universally popular and gradually died out. However in 1939 the minutes of Christ Church's Parochial Church Council noted that 'sittings were not popular and in a great many parishes efforts had been made to free the seats in the church. In Woking it was seen as a valuable and apparently indispensable source of income.'

1940

New council chamber

On 9 January, Woking Council met for the first time in the new chamber at Briarwood in Guildford Road. The previous headquarters had been in Commercial Road and the council had met there for the past thirty-three years. However, to make the councillors feel at home, all the furniture had been moved from the original buildings. Fortunately the new chamber was about the same size as the old one.

Blackout offences

Magistrates at the Woking Petty Sessions held on Saturdays were kept busy during the year fining Woking residents who dared to show, after dark, the tiniest crack of light. The ARP wardens who patrolled the streets were very strict and no excuses were accepted.

Lawrence Poulter of Knaphill was fined ten shillings and grumpily told the magistrates, 'I'd just come home and I was going to bed.' Joseph Mitchell of St John's was fined £1 when he admitted he was drunk and hadn't realised light from his house was shining across his garden and onto the main road.

Compulsory billeting

The billeting officer was not popular when she called on local residents to discover what accommodation was available for evacuees. Because taking in evacuees had at first been voluntary, householders objected to being forced to give details of their houses; they regarded it as undemocratic but more accommodation was needed and they had to comply.

Royal visit

On Saturday, 4 May Her Royal Highness Princess Helena Victoria visited St

John's. The occasion was the opening of a new YMCA hut, which was to be exclusively for the use of young men and women from the armed forces.

Princess Helena, who had opened the YMCA headquarters in Woking in 1930, was handed the key to the new building, which was to be named after her; she then unlocked the door and led the way into the spacious hall, which had a stage at one end. The distinguished guests took their places on the platform and the national anthem was sung. After the Princess had unfurled the Union Jack, a cheque for £1,000 for the organisation was presented to her by Mr Frank Derry, the chairman of the YMCA.

National day of prayer

On Sunday, 26 May the King called for a day of prayer throughout the Empire. In Woking there were large congregations in every church and chapel on that day. In his sermon at Christ Church the vicar, Clifford Banham, said, 'Prayer is not an attempt to get God to do our will, but . . . an attempt to get God's will done by us . . . and that is why I feel today, we can, without reservation or hesitancy, pray to God for victory.'

Dunkirk

In June, crowds thronged Woking station to welcome troops who had been rescued at Dunkirk. As the first trains carrying them arrived at Woking on their way to London, the news spread fast and people flocked to the Broadway – the road beside the railway line – to cheer. About twenty trains a day passed through Woking during that week.

The men were exhausted after their ordeal and Woking residents did their best to provide some relief for them. At first it was private individuals who produced hot drinks, food and cigarettes but then the services of the YMCA were enlisted; with volunteer helpers they were kept busy serving.

Some of the men were from Woking and the surrounding districts so they were able to send reassuring messages to their families on postcards that were provided by the volunteers. Nearly 4,000 of these were used every day. One young soldier preferred to send a verbal message. 'Please go to Courtney Road and tell mother I'm all right,' he begged a local councillor who smilingly agreed. Other volunteers sent telephone messages all over the country on behalf of the troops. Mr Burchett from Westfield was standing on the bridge at Mayford when he suddenly heard a voice shout, 'Hullo, Dad.' His son was on the train.

The troops were so grateful that they gave the volunteers whatever souvenirs they had. Foreign coins were the most common but one lady was given a French helmet, which she proudly wore about the town. Some local residents were able to act as interpreters for the foreign troops. When the French soldiers finally arrived home, they broadcast a message of thanks to the people of Woking.

Vicar removed body

In August, the vicar of St John's, Howard Edmonds, was summonsed for removing a body from the churchyard without a licence. Michael Blumer, who was only sixteen months, had died on 9 June. The following day his father spoke to the vicar and chose a site for his son's grave. The funeral took place on 11 June and Michael was laid to rest in the churchyard.

However, the grave was not exactly where Mr Blumer had specified and he complained to the vicar who said he was sure this could be rectified; he would have the body removed and reburied in the correct site. This he did on 19 June.

But he had broken the law. It was necessary to obtain permission to remove a body after it had been buried and the vicar had to appear in court. Fortunately the magistrates were sympathetic and realised he had acted in good faith so the case was dismissed on payment of costs.

1941

Another blackout offence

Blackout regulations were still causing problems. Any chink of light that might be used by the German pilots to guide their bombs was anathema to the wardens and the police.

On 11 February a constable saw a bright red light in a ground-floor window in Hook Heath. He immediately rang the bell to summon the occupant of the house. The elderly householder, a Miss Holie, was very apologetic. Apparently her maid had had the day off, and she had not realised that the red blind was too thin to blot out the light. She had omitted to draw the blackout curtain. She told the constable she had only recently moved to the house and had not realised she should have drawn it. The constable was not impressed.

Neither was the court. Miss Holie was fined forty shillings for her misdemeanour.

Mr Quartermaine dies

Mr Henry Quartermaine died on 13 February at his home in Guildford Road.

He was seventy-two and had been a successful businessman, a magistrate and chairman of the local council. In 1940 he and his wife had celebrated their golden wedding. He left a widow, two daughters and three grandchildren. One of the latter was Joyce Pearce who later founded the Ockenden Venture.

Mr Quartermaine had lived in Woking for forty-eight years. He was an electrical engineer and had opened the first garage in Woking in Chobham Road. In the first world war it had been commandeered as a munitions work so Mr Quartermaine concentrated on making shells for large guns. He also pioneered the taxi service in Woking and owned a fleet of ten taxis.

Woking's first cinema, which later became the Plaza, was built by him and he had been a member of Woking Council for twenty years, attending his last meeting in June 1941. He was buried in Brookwood cemetery after a well-attended funeral service in Christ Church.

Is that seat free?

Reverend Sanderson of All Saints Church, Woodham, was disturbed about the system of members of the congregation paying to reserve seats in his church. He felt it was 'unthinkable that they should have to pay to worship God'. It created 'a subtle sense of distinction in a place of worship' for all men were equal in the sight of God.

He raised the issue at the annual church meeting, pointing out that the rented seats were often left empty and could not be used by other members of the congregation, who had to squeeze into the 'free' seats. He also felt that the antiquated system discouraged some people from attending church. The meeting agreed with him and the motion to abolish the 'letting' system in Woodham was passed by a large majority.

Lady in grey

Mrs Vera Norwood lived in Rose Cottage next door to the Robin Hood Inn in Knaphill. Originally it had been a sweet shop and an elderly lady was supposed to have died in one of the bay windows. She was so attached to the place that, according to local legend, she frequently returned to haunt it.

Mrs Norwood was sceptical about the tales until one night when she was in bed; her week-old baby was in a cot beside her. To her horror, she suddenly heard the door opening; footsteps came towards her and the cot was pushed forward. Terrified, she burrowed under the bedclothes until she heard the door shut again.

A few days later, Johnny Hunt, a friend of the family, stayed the night. He slept in a bed in the exact spot where the bay window had once been. Mrs Norwood and her husband were suddenly awakened by an unearthly scream.

Rushing into Hunt's room they found him almost incoherent with fear. He swore that a woman wearing a grey cape and bonnet had tried to strangle him. He refused to stay another moment in the cottage and Mr Norwood had to take him back to his lodgings in the middle of the night.

1942

Danger points

In 1941 the Firefighting Act was passed by Parliament and a firewatching scheme, which included enrolled fireguards, came into force. A number of fireguards were appointed in Woking.

One of the fireguards appointed was Mr Vincent Field, who lived in Orchard Drive. He kept a detailed record of his area including 'danger points'. In September he sent the following reports to the head fireguard:

Wheatsheaf Hotel
This building is very well equipped with fire-fighting apparatus and all reasonable precautions appear to have been taken by the management.

Danger Points
The South West Annexe has a flat concrete roof and there is no means of access to it from the inside. This roof is at least thirty feet from the ground but no ladder of that length is available on the premises or for that matter in the whole of the sector.

There is also a definite danger point in the old squash courts. These are now used for storing pockets of hops which, of course, are dry and highly flammable. Several thousand logs of wood have also been piled up against one side of the courts. Should a fire start in the courts, Stirrup Pumps would obviously be quite inadequate although the courts are fairly well away from the main structure. The manager informed me that six members of the staff were prepared to man the Stirrup Pumps and he would be glad if some training could be given.

Kilronan, Horsell Rise
This is an evacuation home for children between the ages of two and five and is run by the 'Waifs and Strays Society'. There is plenty of sand and water buckets have been provided; there are also chemical extinguishers on all floors. There is also a Stirrup Pump in the porch and a fire escape on the top floor.

Danger Points
There are a lot of odd roof spaces as this is a gabled house and access to these is very difficult. In most cases there is only a small trap door in the wall.

Graylands, Chobham Road
This is a large private house standing in its own grounds. There seems to be plenty of water available for fire-fighting. Stirrup Pumps and several water buckets are ready while there is a forty gallon galvanised cask on wheels outside the front door. There are also two pumps in the garden which I was informed are in working order.

As a last line of defence, there is a fair-sized goldfish pond in the garden.

Spy in the workforce

Methold's garage, which had been created to cater for the motorist at work and leisure, now rallied to help the war effort. Petrol was rationed so motoring for pleasure was virtually a thing of the past and consequently there was little repair work needed. Methold's reorganised the business. They installed new lathes and milling machines and proceeded to produce aircraft parts, which were distributed around the country to the larger factories making aircraft and weapons. The name of the company was changed to Methold Engineering Limited. Montague Methold – whose wife, Sybil, had started the original service station in 1927 – used his expertise to help in the high-precision manufacture of bombsight parts.

The workforce consisted of two men, both skilled machinists, and about sixteen women, some of whom were of foreign extraction. All were vetted by the labour exchange before being sent to work for Methold's, which was now involved in the fight to defeat the Germans.

However, one female worker managed to escape the security net; fortunately her arrogance and talkativeness became her downfall. There were two shifts. The day shift ran from six in the morning until two in the afternoon and the night shift was from two until ten at night. One evening when the night shift was almost over, Montague Methold, who was working in his office, was called by a distraught foreman. Two of the women had had an argument and a fight had broken out. The foreman said he could not separate them and needed help. Montague rushed to help and the two women were held until the police arrived.

The argument had started because one of the foreign workers had scoffed at the idea that there were concentration camps in Germany. She considered the idea preposterous. One of her fellow workers, also foreign, took exception to this remark, announcing that there certainly *were* concentration camps in Germany as she had been in one. To prove it she displayed the mark on her arm, which had been branded onto the flesh. When her tormentor still refused to believe her, the concentration-camp victim flew at her and a vicious fight ensued.

The police removed both women and the rest of the workforce, who had been enjoying the spectacle, went home. Because of the blackout and the lack of transport, Montague Methold had to escort some of the women to their residences.

Neither of the assailants appeared for work the next day but the police paid a visit. They informed the Metholds that only one of the two women would be returning. They could still employ the woman who claimed to have been in a concentration camp. The other one, however, would be detained, probably 'during His Majesty's pleasure'. Methold Engineering Limited might be only a small company but Hitler had considered it important enough to put a spy in its midst.

1943

Bored prisoners escape

Fred Sowman, who worked as a cowman on Guinness Dairy farm at Hoe Bridge, found more than cows early one morning when he arrived for work. He told a workmate, Alfred Saunders, 'Someone's been having a nice doss in our hayrick.'

The two men prodded the hay and touched something hard. It was a boot, which was attached to a man who sat up, shook off the hay and glared at them. When another man appeared beside the first, the farm workers were suspicious and rushed to find the farm secretary, Mr Bracey. By the time they returned, the hayrick was empty so Mr Bracey drove his car out of the farm and along Carters Lane. It was not long before he saw two ragged individuals hurrying along the road.

Sure they were German, he apprehended them and called the police. He said later that they had behaved 'like truant schoolboys'. This was not surprising as it appeared they were prisoners of war who had escaped from a train that was taking them to a camp. They told the police that they had been treated well but had escaped because they were 'bored'. They intended to find an aerodrome and steal a plane to fly back to Germany. They assured the police that English POWs were also treated well. They had been free for twelve hours and it was not until the train from Waterloo reached its destination that their disappearance was discovered. They remained at the police station until the military authorities arrived and then left to return to the 'sheer boredom' of their imprisonment.

Pigeon messenger

The Woking target for the 'Wings for Victory' campaign was £600,000. At the start of the campaign in March, a number of pigeons were released in London bearing 'good luck' messages. One of these found its way to Woking.

Stolen rations

In March, Mata Ferrier was sent to prison for two months by Woking magistrates. She had been found guilty of having *five* ration books in different names. She was living in the Farm hotel, in Triggs Lane, Woking. Although she was German by birth, she had married an Englishman so her nationality was British.

When the police searched her room, they found the five ration books, all of which had been used. Mrs Ferrier said she had 'found' them but the police did not believe her and charged her with having 'unlawfully retained more than one ration book without authority'. The magistrates decided that she was intelligent and knew she was breaking the law. It was later discovered that she was an undischarged bankrupt.

Welcome home

On Easter Monday, Send village had cause to rejoice. Private Herbert Darling, who was twenty-four, had been a prisoner in Italy for two years. He was one of the many who had been evacuated from Dunkirk in 1940, but had been taken prisoner by the Italians the following year. On Easter Monday he was repatriated and returned home to general rejoicing.

Sergeant Harvey Macdonald, a former pupil at Woking County School, also arrived home under the repatriation scheme. He nearly didn't make it: the train on which he and other prisoners were being taken to freedom narrowly missed being bombed by the RAF! Sergeant Macdonald said they had waited in a tunnel until the bombing had stopped. When it ceased, they realised the railway line behind them had been blown up.

Wings for victory

At the end of May, four months of preparation culminated in the 'Wings for Victory' week when it was hoped to raise £600,000 to buy planes and equipment to help the war effort. On Saturday, 29 May, a procession, nearly two miles long and led by the band of the Military School of Music, marched through the town from Victoria Arch to the Boys' County Secondary School where Air Vice-Marshal Saunders took the salute. Thousands had gathered along the route to watch and cheer.

During the following week there was entertainment and a number of displays on Wheatsheaf Common. In pride of place was the target indicator, which had been lent to Woking for the occasion. Every few moments it showed a pilot raising his hand in the famous victory sign before releasing a bomb. As the savings total increased, the bombs became larger. On the first day, £117,500 was raised.

The Woking Electric Company's showroom in Chobham Road also housed a fascinating exhibition, called Bomb Berlin. It had been organised by the Electric Company's chief engineer, Mr Fitzroy. Mr Mugford, a local resident, had made a scale model of Berlin out of salvage and for a small fee the public could 'bomb' Berlin from the air with spent electric light bulbs. The most popular targets were the homes of Hitler and Goebbels.

On the following Sunday, 30 May, a drumhead service was held on Wheatsheaf Common. All local churches were represented and thanks were given to God for the success of the RAF in the Battle of Britain. After the service, there was a concert by the RAMC Band. It was one of the most memorable weeks in Woking's history and the town exceeded its target by raising £679,875.

Gordon Boys' School

It was decided that, in future, the name of the 'home' established in memory of General Gordon, should be the Gordon Boys' *School* not *Home*.

1944

Dame Ethel Smyth

On 8 May Dame Ethel Smyth died at her home in Hook Heath. She was eighty-six. Her house was named Coign and she had lived there for over thirty years. She was born in London on 23 April 1858 and studied music at the University of Leipzig. She moved to Woking at the beginning of the twentieth century and became involved in the town's musical activities. She was a patron of the Woking Choral Society and the Woking Musical Society, now no longer in existence. During her lifetime she was a well-known composer who wrote operas and chamber music; on many occasions she conducted performances of her own works in the town. The last time was in 1936.

Ethel Smyth was also a suffragette and in 1911 she combined her two interests by composing *The March of the Women*, which was performed in January of the same year in London. However, she was no passive suffragette and the following year she proved her militancy by smashing windows in the West End of London. She was arrested and given a two-month prison sentence but was released after serving five weeks due to ill health. She had been in Holloway prison long enough to form a critical opinion of the penal system, which she described as 'stupid and brutal'.

She particularly resented the fact that suffragettes were not accorded their rights as 'political prisoners' but were treated worse than criminals. When interviewed by the *Woking News and Mail* after her release, she quoted Mrs Pankhurst's memorable comment. 'Men must either do us justice or do us violence.' The violence referred to was, of course, the forced feeding of suffragettes who had gone on hunger strike. Dr Smyth was not subjected to that indignity but said that she would have liked to have had 'the horrible honour of sharing the sufferings of those women', whom she described as 'heroic'. She was very friendly with the famous Pankhursts and on one occasion Emmeline Pankhurst was arrested outside Ethel Smyth's house in Hook Heath.

Ethel Smyth was created a Dame in 1922 and should certainly be remembered in the town where she lived most of her life and where she died.

Absent without leave

At the beginning of January, William Tedder, a lorry driver from Chobham, was fined by magistrates at the Woking Petty Sessions for being absent from Home Guard duties on several occasions.

Mr Tedder had plenty of excuses. He said he had to walk a mile and a half to the Home Guard headquarters to look at the notice board to see when he was on duty. He also said that he was having medical treatment and was unfit. A doctor, called as a witness, said he was perfectly fit. Mr Tedder thought of another excuse. He was too exhausted to go on parade. His wife corroborated this; she told the magistrates that sometimes her husband was too tired to undress himself and she had to help him. The magistrates were not impressed and Mr Tedder tried again.

When he had to sleep in the hut on duty, he stated, it had been filled with smoke and the blankets were dirty. He complained that he acquired sores on his neck as a result. Lieutenant Rolph, of the same Home Guard company, was outraged; he informed the court that the sleeping quarters were very good. There was adequate lighting and the bedding was clean. It was the first complaint he had received. Tedder had already been fined for a similar offence in August 1943 but he was aggrieved when found guilty again. He refused to pay the £6 fine and said he was going to appeal.

Plane crash

On 30 January two members of the Army Cadet Force were walking near the Six Cross Roads. Hearing a plane circling overhead, they looked up to see a plane with smoke billowing out from its tail. As they watched in horror, it burst into flames and plummeted to the ground, landing on nearby Horsell Common. The two men rushed towards it but the heat was too intense for them to get near. One of the occupants had been hurled out by the explosion and lay on his back some distance from the burning wreck.

The body of the other occupant was badly charred and he was already dead. The first one died later in hospital. The two men were identified as the First Officer, Stanley Herringshaw and the Engineer Officer, Stanley Cooke, both of the Air Transport Auxiliary. At the inquest, John Crowther of Ottershaw, a senior examiner from the Aeronautical Inspection Department, said the plane had been fit to fly although Mr Cooke's brother disputed this. The coroner, however, accepted the findings and recorded a verdict of accidental death.

Oranges delight

In February, for the first time in years, fresh oranges were on sale in Woking. As the news spread, queues formed outside greengrocers early on the Monday morning. The official ration was one pound per ration book; this amounted to four oranges. By midday the shops were sold out and women proudly carried home their baskets of oranges while children sucked their fruit in the street.

News from Normandy

In August Sergeant Pollard, serving with the British Army in Normandy, wrote to his parents in Woking:

> We drove Jerry back so fast that the French people in the villages did not have time to move out. Jerry went back . . . on anything he could get away on with speed. They were having a meal in one house and did not stop to finish it. . . . We passed by the grave of a German soldier buried by the roadside. A cross bore his name and age (15 years). I have seen hundreds of prisoners during the last few days. They seem to be boys looking very sorry for themselves.

1945

VE Day

German forces unconditionally surrendered to the Allied Expeditionary Force in the early hours of Monday, 7 May and news of the ceasefire was passed to the troops at the front. The official ending of hostilities was one minute after midnight on Tuesday, 8 May, which was declared VE (Victory in Europe) Day.

Thousands of people listened to the broadcast by Winston Churchill, the prime minister, announcing the end of the war:

> The German War is now at an end. . . . We may allow ourselves a brief period

of rejoicing; but let us not forget for a moment the toil and efforts that lie ahead. Japan, with all her treachery and greed, remains unsubdued. . . . Advance Britannia. Long live the cause of freedom. God save the King.

His words were followed with a fanfare by buglers of the Scots Guards.

Woking, with the rest of the country, rejoiced. Two days' public holiday was declared and the schools were closed. Food shops opened until about half past nine and crowds flocked to buy enough supplies for the two days. Bunting and flags appeared miraculously in the streets. Most residents found something in the appropriate colours with which to decorate their houses. Adults wore red, white and blue rosettes and children wore the same colour ribbons. The church bells of St Peter's, Old Woking, and St Mary's, Horsell, pealed out, and packed congregations in all the churches attended special services of thanksgiving.

Later, impromptu street parties took place in many areas, bonfires were lit and effigies of Hitler were burnt. In Kingfield, the mothers decided to give the children a street party they would never forget. They pooled resources, made sandwiches and baked cakes. Beaconsfield Road was decorated with patriotic bunting and long tables were set up there; these were tastefully decorated with vases of red, white and blue flowers from the local gardens.

Seventy children sat down to tea and were waited on by their parents. Afterwards each child was presented with a book containing a 'savings stamp', an orange and a packet of sweets. Many residents had generously given up their sweet ration to provide a treat for the children. After tea there were races and games on Kingfield Green and a huge bonfire was lit. The crowds, including two passing soldiers, cheered as an effigy of Hitler, tied to a stake, was hurled on to the flames. Fireworks ended a day that the children would long remember.

Elsewhere there had also been celebrations. A two-hour extension was granted to all pubs for VE Day only, so they stayed open until midnight. At nine o'clock in the evening the King broadcast a message to all his subjects. Crowds gathered outside the Albion Hotel to listen to it through the loudspeakers and then stayed to dance to music until the small hours.

After years of blackout, lights blazed in the streets and from buildings. Red, blue and white fairy-lights were popular and St Mary's church in Horsell was floodlit for the first time in years. Searchlights swept the skies in celebration – no longer searching for enemy aircraft.

Victory parade

The following Sunday an impressive victory parade was held. All local groups and services were represented and a crowd of about ten thousand packed the streets. The parade assembled in Guildford Road and, led by the band of the

RAMC, marched to the old council offices in Commercial Road where representatives of the council, education bodies and magistrates joined in. The procession was entirely on foot; no vehicles were permitted. It continued its march to Wheatsheaf Common where a service of thanksgiving was held.

Clementine calls

In June, Mrs Clementine Churchill, wife of the prime minister, visited Woking to receive purses containing money raised by the Woking and District appeal on behalf of the YWCA. Mrs Churchill was the president of the YWCA wartime appeal. Wearing a black hat and coat – decorated only with a pearl necklace and a large white flower – she received a rapturous reception from Woking residents. She inspected the guard of honour comprising YWCA juniors, club members, nurses, service women, the Women's Land Army, Guides and Brownies.

She was then escorted to Christ Church hall where she was told that the target of £5,000 had been exceeded. Half of the money raised would go to her wartime appeal and the other half would be used for the local YMCA work.

1946

New loos

In January the council decided that the two air-raid shelters in Commercial Road and Chobham Road should be converted into public conveniences.

Demob happy

Soldiers from the Far East and the Middle East who were being 'demobbed' were taken first to Aldershot, the home of the British Army. From there, they travelled to Inkerman Barracks where they were issued with civilian clothes. Then, carrying large kitbags and boxes of 'civvies', they were driven by lorry to Woking station for the final stages of their journey home.

In the station yard the YMCA had set up a mobile canteen. Each man was given a cup of tea, a bun, a bar of chocolate and some cigarettes to sustain him for the journey. Nearly 2,000 men were served every day and 200 telegrams, on behalf of the men, were sent by the YMCA to families around the country. On Saturdays the canteen was transferred to the Grand Hotel where the men arrived about half past nine in the morning. After they had received their goodies, they were driven to the station to catch the special train provided for them.

Cricket sensations

This was the year Alec Bedser made his debut in test cricket. The Bedser twins, Alec and Eric, were born in Woking on 4 July 1918 and became the town's most famous sportsmen. They were educated at Monument Hill school and attended church at All Saints, Woodham, where they sang in the choir. It was not long before their aptitude for the noble game of cricket became apparent.

They played their first match for their county, Surrey, in 1938. Unfortunately, the war broke out in the following year and their careers were put on hold for five years. They were twenty-one and they both served in the RAF. After they were demobbed, it was not long before they reappeared on the cricketing scene and it was Alec who proved to be the better player of the two. A medium-fast bowler, he was selected play for England in the first test against India at Lords in 1946.

During the 1946–7 tour of Australia he bowled the famous Donald Bradman out for a duck. The batsman later said it was the finest ball he had ever had bowled to him. Alec was the first English bowler to take 100 wickets against Australia.

False claim

Residents who had had their houses damaged by bombs were entitled to claim compensation from the War Damage Commission. However, the system was open to abuse. Jim Roberts, a wood merchant and dealer, put in a fraudulent claim. He said that on 23 June 1944 a flying bomb had demolished the caravan in which he was living on Send Hill. He claimed £135 in compensation and produced false documentation to prove his claim. In fact a flying bomb had landed near his home but it had done minimal damage and his caravan had certainly not been destroyed.

In August 1946 Woking magistrates found him guilty of attempting to defraud the commission and fined him £75 with costs of three guineas. He was given twenty-eight days to pay or the option of going to prison for three months.

1947

Alec Bedser

Alec Bedser was named *Wisden* cricketer of the year.

Woking freezes

During February it was bitterly cold. Coal was difficult to obtain and, as most houses were heated with coal fires, many householders were forced to switch to electricity. Unfortunately the increased load on the supply caused a dramatic power cut for nearly four hours one morning.

The winter of 1947 was to be one of the coldest on record. The frozen Basingstoke canal became a popular skating rink and the deep snow, while dangerous for drivers and pedestrians, provided children with plenty of opportunity for snowball fights.

Royal Military Police

At the end of July the Military Police held a 'corps' week to celebrate the granting of the Royal prefix. In future they would be known as the *Royal* Military Police. A ceremonial parade was held at Inkerman Barracks to inaugurate the week and the Duke of Gloucester took the salute.

D.I.Y.

It was becoming increasingly difficult for ex-servicemen to find accommodation for themselves and their families. So many houses had been destroyed and the building of new properties was just beginning.

Having been demobbed from the RAMC in 1945, Joseph Timmins was becoming desperate to find somewhere to live. Eventually he decided the only way to get over the difficulty was to build a house himself. So he bought a plot of land in Horsell. Before the war he had been a bricklayer so his skills were put to good use. It took him twelve months to complete an attractive, detached house with three bedrooms. He was so pleased with his efforts that he built a similar house next door for his brother-in-law.

Royal wedding

On Thursday, 30 November Princess Elizabeth married Prince Philip at Westminster Abbey. Many Woking residents were able to hear the service broadcast on the wireless but some lucky viewers watched it on black-and-white television.

The Princess and her new husband were to honeymoon in Romsey at the home of Prince Philip's uncle, Lord Mountbatten, and the royal train passed through Woking in the evening on its way to Winchester. There was a huge demand for platform tickets and crowds packed the station platforms. Those who could not get onto the station thronged Broadway beside the railway line. The front of the royal train was illuminated and decorated. As dark fell, it travelled through the station at a greater speed than anticipated so unfortunately there was no chance to catch a glimpse of the newlyweds.

1948

Wedding cake

On Sunday, 8 January a special party was held at the Barrens, White Rose Lane. It was given by the officers and crew of SRS *Wakefield*. They were one of the nineteen Sea Ranger crews recognised by the Admiralty. The party was to celebrate the presentation of a piece of Princess Elizabeth's wedding cake to the crew.

Triumph at Boys' School

At the end of March the Woking Boys' Secondary School – now known as the Boys' Grammar School – performed Shakespeare's great play, *The Merchant of Venice*. The school's dramatic society had been doing productions since 1918 and had an excellent reputation. As in Shakespeare's day, the female roles were played by boys and on this occasion 14-year-old John Cartwright played the part of Portia to great acclaim. The play was directed by one of the masters, Reginald Church, who had directed all the previous plays.

The tickets sold out very quickly and a number of distinguished visitors attended, including a BBC producer and the Norwegian ambassador. The latter attended on the last night and during the Easter holidays the cast of the play, the head and other members of staff took the play to Norway. Four performances were given in the state theatre in Bergen, five in the New Theatre, Oslo, and one in the high school in the mountain village of Voss. The school took its own costumes and props but the scenery was provided by the Norwegians.

They played to packed houses and the first performance in Oslo was attended by Crown Prince Olav and his three children. Other distinguished visitors, including the British, Dutch and American ambassadors, also watched the play. The Norwegians were delighted with the visit and considered the boys extremely well behaved. They were excellent 'ambassadors for England'.

While in Bergen, they met the leader of the wartime resistance movement and also a schoolmistress whose home had been used by the group. After the last performance, Mr Humphreys, the headmaster, addressed the audience. He told them, 'We came as ambassadors of England. We go home as ambassadors of Norway.'

Above left: The Angel of Peace on top of the war memorial.

Above right: St Peter's church, Old Woking, built by King William I on the site of an earlier minster.

Below left: Sir William Grove stands in Woking park admiring the fuel cell.

Below right: General Gordon sits on his camel in the grounds of Gordon's School.

Above:
War memorial in Brookwood cemetery, with names inscribed on the panels.

Below:
The Chobham cannon: a replica of the one presented by the War Office in 1900.

Above:
The 'Old' Girls' Grammar School, 1954.

Below:
The fuel cell, built in 2003 – a first for Woking.

Above left: The Muslim burial ground, erected in 1915.

Above right: The Shah Jehan Mosque, built in 1889.

Below left: The 'Martian Landing', erected in 1998 to celebrate the centenary of *The War of the Worlds* by H. G. Wells.

Below right: The Peacocks, which dates from 1992.

Woking's own Alec Bedser, in 1955. Sir Donald Bradman, the greatest batsman of all time, said that Bedser got him out with the 'finest ball' he ever faced during a test match in Australia in the late 1940s.
(courtesy of Empics)

Local man Chris Chataway – of Shaftesbury Road – was nothing if not versatile. An Oxford Blue he became a world-record holder on the track, a television commentator, an MP and government minister and a successful businessman. He also acted as pacemaker for Roger Bannister during the first sub 4-minute mile (*above*) on 6 May 1954. Chataway is the lead runner.
(courtesy of Empics)

Dr Who and his Dalek. In the 1980s and 1990s Woking's Peter Davison
(*second from right*) starred in hit shows like *Doctor Who*,
All Creatures Great and Small and *A Very Peculiar Practice*.
(courtesy of Mirrorpix)

One of the most influential musicians of the 1980s, Paul Weller, of Sheerwater, formed The Jam and later a new band, The Style Council. He is seen here leading The Style Council at the Live Aid concert at Wembley Stadium in 1985. (courtesy of Mirrorpix)

Landmark removed

In May, James Walker removed the spire that surmounted the clock tower at the entrance to their offices. Unfortunately dry rot had attacked the timber and it had become dangerous. It was therefore taken down in the interests of safety. The spire had been a local landmark since the Royal Dramatic College, over which it had towered, had been opened by the Prince of Wales in 1865. It remained in place when Martinsyde's took over the building in 1915 and James Walker, who acquired the site in 1925, also left it alone.

Although it now had to be removed, James Walker promised that the appearance of the building would be kept as close as possible to the original. The central hall, retaining many of the original features, was used by the firm as a board room.

Smart Alec

Alec Bedser continued his cricketing success. In one of the test matches against South Africa he and his team mate, Gladwin, formed a partnership and scored eight runs in the last over to defeat their opponents by two wickets.

Olympic flame

In August the Olympic flame passed through Woking on its way to the Olympic Games. A 'changeover' took place at the Gordon Boys' School.

Sheerwater

In October, London County Council was concerned about the number of people in London who had been bombed out of their homes during the war. Rebuilding was very slow and they looked for an area outside London where over 1,000 houses could be built. The area chosen was Sheerwater, which stretched from Maybury Hill to West Byfleet. One hundred years ago this area had been a natural lake but, at the beginning of the twentieth century, it had been drained by Lord King of Ockham. But the name remained. 'Sheerwater' means clear water.

London County Council planned to create an estate with houses, schools, churches, recreation grounds, a community centre and, of course, public houses. It would cater for all and would cost £2 million.

1949

Lady Baden-Powell visits

At the end of May, Lady Baden-Powell, the chief guide, visited Woking. The occasion was a rally held in the garden of the Southern Railway Orphanage. She was welcomed by groups of Brownies, Guides and Rangers who later gave displays of their work during the year.

Bedsers visit school

In July Alec and Eric Bedser, the famous cricketing twins, visited their old school, Monument Hill County Secondary, to do the honours at the annual prize-giving. Before handing each book to the prizewinners, they autographed it. They also presented an autographed cricket bat to Robert Carter, the most promising cricketer in the school.

Sweets rationed again

In August sweets were rationed again. When the date was known, queues formed at confectioners as residents were determined to stock up before once again being deprived of their treats. The town of Woking obviously had a collective sweet tooth.

'Making do'

The Woking County Grammar School for Girls was still 'making do' with its primitive accommodation. In September 1949, twenty-eight more girls had been admitted than in the previous year. Miss Hill told the Woking governing body for higher education, 'The problem of accommodation is becoming desperate.'

Memorial Bible

In December a memorial Bible was presented to the Boys' Grammar School by Unwin's, the printers. It was a replica of one that had been commissioned by King George V for the cathedral at Philadelphia. The beautiful binding, reminiscent of the *Codex Sinaiticus* in the British Museum, had been a gift from Leonard Catto. The Bible was reverently placed on the carved-oak lectern in the school hall; this had been installed as a tribute to those Old Boys who had given their lives in the second world war.

1950

First member

In the February general election Woking elected its first MP, as a new Woking constituency had been formed. There were three candidates: Harold Watkinson, Conservative; Trevor Davies, Labour; and Captain Turner Bridges, Liberal. All held meetings and canvassed voters right up to the night before the election, which was held on Thursday, 23 February.

After the polling stations had closed, the sealed ballot boxes were taken to Woking police station where they were locked in cells overnight. The following morning, at eight o'clock, they were taken under police escort to the Boys' Grammar School where counting started in the hall an hour later and continued all day. There was a record number of votes and people started to gather outside the hall to wait for the result at about two o'clock. It was not until five o'clock that the public were allowed into the hall to hear the result. It was given by the returning officer, Captain Neville Lawrence, the High Sheriff of Surrey, who lived in Hookheath. The Conservative, Harold Watkinson, won with a majority of over 11,000. The Liberal candidate lost his deposit.

Maiden speech

Mr Watkinson made his maiden speech in the House of Commons during the defence debate. He had been an engineer and gunnery officer during the war. A graduate of the Naval Gunnery school, he quoted its motto: 'If you want peace, prepare for war.' He said Britain should prepare for the *next* war and not the *last* one. 'We should spend our defences the best way we can by looking forward and trying to perceive the worst that lies before us.'

After he sat down, many MPs from all parties congratulated him and the Prime Minister remarked, 'I thought the speech of the Honourable Member for Woking was very interesting.'

Glades of remembrance

In May the Bishop of Guildford dedicated the glades of remembrance at Brookwood cemetery. They had been designed and laid out by Mr Wilner White as a final resting place for the ashes of the dead. The service was conducted by the vicar of St Johns, Reverend Edmonds. Present were Guy Pritchett, chairman of Woking Council and Roger Pemberton, the chairman of the London Necropolis Company. The latter noted that there was now less prejudice against cremation.

Sheerwater

The plans to create a new community in Sheerwater continued. 210 acres from the end of Eve and Arnold Roads, almost to West Byfleet, had been cleared. Because of the original lake, the ground was still waterlogged and it would take some time to dry out the 'liquid mud'. The layout of the new estate was to be planned in conjunction with Surrey County Council.

Royal Tournament

In June the Gordon Boys' School had the honour of taking part in the Royal Tournament at Earls Court. The display of 'Gordon Cavalry', which was modelled on the Household Cavalry, was given by 118 boys. There were two squadrons, each headed by a 'baron', a 'knight' and a 'rider' and heralded by three trumpets. The school band provided the music. There was great interest in a display of the school's work that was exhibited.

1951

Memorial organ

At the end of January the Boys' Grammar School held a special service in the school hall during the annual Old Wokingians' weekend. On the balcony a pipeless, electronic organ had been installed beneath a memorial window dedicated to Joshua Holden, the first headmaster. The plaque on the organ read: 'This organ was presented to the school by Mrs K. Lester in memory of her son, George Lester, headmaster of the school 1939–42.'

The Bishop of Guildford dedicated the organ and F. A. Woodward – vicar of St Mary's, Horsell and chairman of the governors – led the service. The organ was played by Laurence West, an old Wokingian, who was organist to the King at the Royal Lodge, Windsor, and played for services in St George's Chapel. He played Handel's *Water Music* and selections from Bach and Vaughan Williams.

'The best bowler in the world'

At the end of April a reception was held at Christ Church hall to pay tribute to Alec Bedser. He had recently returned from the MCC cricket tour of Australia where he had been named 'the best bowler in the world'. After the reception, there was a dinner in the Albion Hotel, where the cricketer was presented with a television set, a colour photograph of himself and a cheque for £200. Any extra money that was collected later would be donated to the National Playing Fields Association.

Mr Barrett, chairman of Woking Council, said, 'Truly Alec has brought honour to this town and we in Woking are glad indeed to have this opportunity of welcoming him home and showing our appreciation.' In reply, Bedser reminded his audience that his roots were firmly embedded in Woking. He had been born in Vale Farm Road and his parents had been married in Christ Church. He was particularly delighted with the gift of the television as it would enable his mother to watch her first test match.

Festival of Britain

In May a procession marched from the council offices to the Ritz cinema where a service was held to mark the opening of the Festival of Britain. It was headed by the Salvation Army band, which was followed by members of the council, representatives of youth organisations and local groups and the army cadets.

The headmaster of Charterhouse school in Godalming, Mr Turner, gave the address. He said that although the country was still suffering from the scars of war, it was right that the Festival of Britain should be a celebration and it was appropriate that it should be inaugurated with an act of Christian worship.

Singing success

As part of the Festival of Britain, a National Competitive Music Festival was held in association with the Arts Council of Great Britain. One of the venues was the Royal Festival Hall where a choir festival took place in May. To reach the national finals, choirs from all over England entered local competitions. In the Surrey-area finals of the church-choirs class, held in February, two choirs from Woking took part. These were from the Congregational church and Trinity Methodist. Both had to sing the secular set piece, 'To Music', by Dyson; for their sacred piece the Congregational church choir chose 'Save Us, O Lord' by Bairstow and Trinity Methodist sang Wood's 'Magnificat in D'.

The winners were Trinity Methodist who therefore entered the national final at the Royal Festival Hall. Conducted by Mr F. T. Hilliger, they sang the set piece followed by another version of the *Magnificat* by Walmisley. They were placed seventh out of eleven but they brought glory to the town by reaching the finals.

An OBE for Madame de Lara

Seventy-nine year old Madame Adelina de Lara of Wych Hill, Woking, the celebrated concert pianist, was made an OBE in the King's birthday honours list. On 2 June she opened the Woking Society of Arts exhibition where over one hundred local artists had displayed their work. This too was part of the Festival of Britain.

St Andrew's

During the war a Presbyterian church in Lambeth had been destroyed by a bomb and the War Damage Commission paid for a new church to be built. The Church Extension Committee decided that it was not necessary to build the new church in Lambeth. Woking had a large Presbyterian congregation which, since 1941, had worshipped in the YMCA building every Sunday.

The new church was to be St Andrew's and it would be built at the corner of White Rose Lane and Heathside Road. There was a service at which the foundation stone was laid, followed by a tea in Trinity Methodist hall.

Sheerwater service

Although there was no church on the Sheerwater estate and no residents had moved in, the Woking Methodist circuit held a service on the site of the prospective church. About twenty people attended. When residents moved in, services would be held in the Sorbo Works until a church was built.

In September, Londoners started to move into the new estate. The first couple to take up residence were Mr and Mrs Sewell from Battersea. Their house was at 3 Albert Drive. Mr Sewell's parents lived in New Haw but his wife had never lived anywhere but London and she did not like the 'gnats and crawly things' she found in Sheerwater. Perhaps the erstwhile 'lake' was to blame!

1952

Smart skeleton

At the end of January, two boys walking in West Wycombe made a gruesome discovery. Under a hedge beside the road, they discovered a skeleton still wearing the remains of a brown suit.

The police were alerted and eventually the remains were identified as those of Douglas Rollo Rouse, the 35-year-old manager of the Horsell chemist, Moss's. He had been missing since 30 July 1951 when he had left his home in

Horsell and cycled to the Constitution Club where he had had one drink and was never seen again.

His wife was in no doubt the skeleton was that of her husband because of the signet ring engraved with the initial D. R. R. She had no idea why he should have gone to West Wycombe.

Sheerwater visit

In February Harold Watkinson, the local MP, visited some of the residents on the new Sheerwater estate. He declared it 'one of the best planned estates I have seen'.

Death of George VI

On Wednesday, 13 February King George VI died. Woking Council expressed 'their heartfelt sorrow at the death of their beloved King George VI and tender their deep and respectful sympathy to Her Majesty Queen Elizabeth II, the Queen Mother and other members of the Royal Family and congratulations on Her Majesty's accession to the Throne.'

A memorial service led by the vicar of Christ Church was held on the evening of Friday, 15 February, the day of the funeral, and the congregation numbered nearly eight hundred. The shops had closed at one o'clock as a mark of respect and the muffled bell of St Peter's church was tolled fifty-six times (the King's age). The bell ringer was 77-year-old Mr Grease of Old Woking who had also tolled the bell for three previous monarchs.

St Andrew's dedicated

In February St Andrew's Presbyterian Church held its dedication service, which was led by the Right Reverend Bacon, the moderator of the general assembly of the Presbyterian Church of England. The building was now complete and seated 348 with twenty-four choir stalls.

Olympic Games

In July three Woking athletes took part in the Olympic Games in Helsinki: Bill Nankeville from Horsell ran in the 1,500 metres; Nick Stacey, a former Oxford Blue who also lived in Horsell ran in the 200 metres, the 100-metre relay and the 400-metre relay; Chris Chataway, also an Oxford Blue, from Shaftesbury Road, ran in the 5,000 metres.

Although none of them won, they all gave creditable performances. On their return from Helsinki, they were driven in an open car through cheering crowds to attend an official reception in Christ Church hall followed by a welcome-home dinner at the Albion Hotel.

Sheerwater church

The church of St Michael and All Saints in Sheerwater was open for the first time in May. The Bishop of Guildford consecrated the altar and dedicated the church and hall.

1953

Posterity postbox

In February it was suggested to Woking Council that, as part of the coronation celebrations, Woking should have a 'posterity postbox'. Letters from a selection of Woking residents would be posted into a specially designed postbox, which would be opened fifty years hence in 2003. The cost was estimated at £200 and it was hoped that it would be a permanent memorial of the coronation.

In March it was agreed in principle that the 'posterity postbox' should go ahead and it would probably be sited in Woking Park. The first letter would be posted by a famous person at three o'clock on the afternoon of 27 May and the ceremony would be filmed so that it could be watched in 2003 by future Woking residents. The film could be distributed to cinemas throughout the country and the idea would 'put Woking on the map'. Mr Bishop, whose idea it was, said he would organise it; designs for the postbox had already been submitted.

Then came the blow. At the next meeting, the council decided not to proceed with the idea. Some members felt £200 was too much to spend on a project that did not have general support. Those in favour of the scheme pointed out that the council had already voted to spend £1,200 on flags and bunting and £750 on coronation mugs for the children. The majority was not impressed by this argument and the fascinating idea of a posterity postbox died. What a shame!

Chataway wins mile

In March, Chris Chataway won the mile event at the university sports at White City. For the last 250 yards he was running against a strong wind. His time was just over four minutes and he became the third fastest British miler after Roger Bannister and Sydney Wooderson.

Coronation day

At seven o'clock on the morning of the coronation, 78-year-old George Cole rang the bell of St Peter's church. Queen Elizabeth II was the fourth monarch for whom he had done this. Bunting decorated the roads and railway bridges and flags adorned the lamp-posts; a representation of Woking's coat of arms laid out in flowers had been created in Woking Park.

In the afternoon over 12,000 people thronged the streets to watch the two processions. The first one left Wheatsheaf Common at two o'clock. A single police motorcyclist led the way and the procession, which was in three sections, was headed by the band of the Royal Army Medical Corps. This was followed by representatives of the services including the Old Contemptibles, the Military Police and the Home Guard. Then came the Salvation Army at the head of the youth groups, and the procession ended with the competitors for the fancy-dress competition. The head of the procession arrived in Woking Park at half past two when an aerial maroon was fired. From a dais, Mr Darby, chairman of Woking Council, took the salute.

The second procession of decorated vehicles assembled in Sheerwater and paraded through the town. Prizes were awarded for the most imaginative. The first prize was given to a 50-year-old pony trap drawn by a 3-year-old pony, Flash, and decorated in red, white and blue. The second and third prizes both went to bicycles. The second was a tandem ridden by Mr and Mrs Stimson; it was also decorated in the national colours. The third prize went to 73-year old cyclist Barry West who bore in front of him a shield decorated with the St George Cross surmounted with patriotic flags.

Later, in Woking Park, 1,500 balloons were released and the celebrations lasted until midnight ending with the inevitable firework display.

New girls' school

In June the ministry of education accepted the recommendation of Surrey County Council that building plans for 1954–5 should include a new girls' grammar school.

1954

Community spirit

In February a community centre was opened in Sheerwater by the Lord Lieutenant, General Sir Robert Haining. He said the new building should be used for a variety of purposes.

Getting his feet under the table

On the evening of 6 March Mrs Lillian Burge, the housekeeper of a residence in Kettlewell Hill, filled a hot-water bottle in the kitchen. As this caused the room to steam up, she opened a window before taking the bottle upstairs. When she came down, she heard a noise in the kitchen and went to investigate. A man's legs were sticking out from under the table! When she asked him what he was doing, he 'just grunted'. Grabbing a broom, she brandished it at him and he fled out of the back door.

Her husband chased him down Chobham Road but lost him in Wheatsheaf Close. Later, 41-year-old Jack Randall was arrested by the police and charged with 'intent to commit a felony'. He denied the charge but Mrs Burge identified him and he was sent for trial at the Surrey Quarter Sessions.

Stowaway

On 23 March, Iris Weagle landed at Salford docks and made her way to her mother's home in Courtney Road, Woking. In 1945 she had married a Canadian and gone to Canada to live but the marriage had broken up two years' later. For the next five years she worked hard to keep herself but was very homesick.

In March she met two of the crew from the ship *Isa Carter*, which was bound for England. They smuggled her aboard and hid her in the crew's quarters but she was discovered. She was allowed to return to Woking but had to appear before the Woking magistrates who fined her £5. She was given six months to pay and she told them she was very glad to be home. The two crew members were also fined for aiding and abetting a stowaway.

Queen Mum visits Wisley

In August the Queen Mother visited Wisley. It was the 150th anniversary of the founding of the Royal Horticultural Society and the fiftieth anniversary of Wisley gardens. She was accompanied by her brother, David Bowes-Lyon, who was president of the society. The Queen Mother opened a new students' hostel and planted a tree to commemorate her visit.

Alec Bedser

Alec Bedser followed some of the greatest names in cricket when he was appointed senior professional in the forthcoming MCC party to tour Australia.

1955

Golden jubilee for Trinity Methodist

In January Trinity Methodist church celebrated its golden jubilee. At the conference the principal guest was the president of the Methodist Conference, Reverend Russell Shearer. In the chair was Maurice Prior, who was the grandson of King Prior, the first minister of the church. A commemoration service was held on the Sunday.

Guildford Cathedral

Guildford diocese was created in 1927 and the foundation stone of the Cathedral had been laid in 1936 but it was still not completed and more money was needed. During Guildford Cathedral week in January, Woking hoped to raise £2,500 towards the cost of the building. The town set itself a task to sell bricks at two shillings and sixpence each to every man, woman and child in the district. There were a million bricks for sale and, if they were all sold, £175,000 would be raised. The chairman of Woking Council, Robert Beldam, wrote an appeal in the local paper pleading with its readers to 'be a brick' and 'be a builder'.

The Ockenden Venture

In April, the Ockenden Venture was launched when Joyce Pearce took five refugee children into her home in Ockenden, White Rose Lane. Earlier she had visited displaced persons' camps in West Germany and been moved by the plight of the children, many of whom had lost parents during the war. She aimed to give them a good education and a stable home in the United Kingdom.

The first girls, aged between twelve and fifteen, came from behind the Iron Curtain – from the Ukraine, Poland, Latvia and Lithuania. They would be educated at Greenfield School and an appeal was launched for funds. £225 had already been received anonymously.

Going back in time

The Christ Church clock was obviously affected by the cold weather as for several days it decided to go backwards to the confusion of passers-by! That was not the only problem for the town church. During the Christmas period some daring individual had removed the weathervane from the spire. It was not recovered by the police until the end of January when it was put back in its customary place and the clock was persuaded to move in the right direction.

Sheerwater shops

In February the first shop, a butcher's, opened in Sheerwater. This was quickly followed by others to form a small shopping centre on the new estate.

Pilgrimage to Guildford

On Palm Sunday, a beautiful sunny day, there was a pilgrimage to Guildford Cathedral, which was attended by Princess Margaret. The chairman of Woking Council, Mr Beldame, and the deputy clerk, Mr Shawcross, took part in the procession and coach loads from Woking were driven to Guildford after their morning services. Other residents made their own way by car, public transport or even bicycle.

The first part of the procession followed the mediaeval pattern and pilgrims, garbed appropriately, followed the cross. Behind them came pilgrims dressed in the modern style; 15,000 people attended the pilgrimage. The afternoon service, led by the Bishop, lasted for thirty-five minutes and ended with an act of affirmation.

New colour for Gordon's

In July the Duke of Edinburgh presented a second colour to Gordon's Boys' School. The first colour had been given to the school by Dr Hope in 1895 and before the start of every Sunday morning service, the colour was laid on the altar.

The Duke, wearing the uniform of a field marshal, was escorted to the dais by Admiral of the Fleet, Viscount Cunningham, who was chairman of governors. It was the first time the consort of a reigning monarch had visited the school and many local VIPs were present.

The old colour was paraded around the ground dipping in salute to the Duke. It was then carried into the school and the doors closed behind it. The new colour was handed to the Duke by Major Edwards of the cadet corps and he presented it to Sergeant Turnbull and the trooping of the colour took place.

At the service that followed, the new colour was consecrated by the Bishop of Guildford and the service ended with the school prayer.

Last test

Alec Bedser played his last test match against South Africa.

Record breaker

On August bank holiday, in front of a 40,000 crowd at White City, Woking athlete Chris Chataway broke the world record for the three-mile event.

1956

First wedding

On 11 February Jennifer Nottingham married Captain William Hill in the chapel of St Edward the Confessor at Gordon's Boys' School. It was an historic occasion as it was the first time a wedding had been performed in the chapel. The bride's father was Brigadier Nottingham, the commandant of the Gordon's Boys, and a special licence had to be obtained from the Archbishop of Canterbury as the chapel was not licensed for weddings.

The bride wore cream brocade and her three bridesmaids wore pale-pink jackets over blue velvet dresses. The service was conducted by Reverend Alec Giles, the school chaplain, and the bridegroom's brother officers formed a guard of honour as the couple emerged from the chapel.

Out of breath

One of the productions put on by Horsell Amateur Dramatic Society was *Blithe Spirit* by Noel Coward. One of the actresses was Susan Chataway, the sister of Chris. He was in the audience and laughed when she came rushing on to the stage – out of breath from running.

Helicopter garden party

At the end of July an unusual garden party was held in the grounds of Dunsborough House in Ripley. It was the first-ever *helicopter* garden-party. Ten helicopters carrying 250 guests landed in the grounds. Among the visitors were Donald Campbell, the racing driver, and Tyrone Power, the Hollywood film star.

Champions

Alec and Eric Bedser played their part in helping Surrey to their fifth county championship. Stuart Surridge, the captain, paid tribute to Eric. He said, 'I don't know what we'd have done without Eric Bedser. He bowled his off-spinners brilliantly.'

1957

Harold promotes Harold

In January, Harold Watkinson, MP for Woking, became a member of the Cabinet. He had been Minister of Transport and Civil Aviation since 1955 but the new Prime Minister, Harold Macmillan, decided to include the department in the Cabinet.

Playing for England

In February two young men from Woking, John Mortimore and Geoff Harrison, were chosen to play for England against Wales in the amateur soccer international at Peterborough on 16 February.

Ideal home

In March a house in Woking was chosen as house of the year by *Ideal Home* magazine. Owned by Mr Broderick, the Hookheath house, named Breeze, was built in a T-shape on two levels; electricity was mainly used for heating but there was also an experiment in thermal insulation. It had been designed by the owner in cooperation with the architect, Mr Lesley Gooday.

Coco the Clown

The children of Woking had a treat one Saturday morning when they watched Coco the Clown from Bertram Mills circus clumping down Chobham Road in his size twenty-four boots. He was on his way to the Ritz cinema where he performed to the delight of the young audience.

Pub for Sheerwater

In June Sheerwater opened its first public house, the Birch and Pines.

Parachute jump

In the same month, above Fairoaks aerodrome in Chobham, James Basnett of the British Parachute Club jumped from an Auster aircraft from a height of 2,000 feet and delayed opening his parachute for seven seconds. The event was the first of its kind to be broadcast by the BBC Light Programme.

Golden jubilee

Saturday, 6 July was a memorable one for Brooklands. On that day Lord Brabazon unveiled a golden jubilee memorial. It was the fiftieth anniversary of the first race meeting to be held at Brooklands and Brabazon had taken part in the first race. Many famous cars that had raced at Brooklands emerged from obscurity and made their appearance, as did many old motorcycles.

Aga Khan

On 21 August the Aga Khan attended a memorial service for his late grandfather at the Shah Jehan Mosque. The Queen had recently bestowed on him the title of Highness. She was represented at the ceremony by the Earl of Scarborough, who was received by the Aga Khan when he arrived at the mosque.

About three hundred guests attended the service, which was led by the Imam, Muhammad Yahya Butt. One of the guests was Sir Francis Low, a friend of the Aga Khan, who had been the editor of *The Times of India* before retiring to Woking in 1948.

Open day

On 23 October an open day was held at the Church Army home in Coley Avenue. The former home of Wilson Carlile, the founder of the Church Army, it had been opened earlier in the summer as a 'Short Stay Sunset Home for the aged and infirm'. The home would later be known as the Marie Carlile Church Army Home after Wilson Carlile's sister, who lived with him. At the open day, the matron, Miss Cotgreave, showed the visitors round; they were impressed with the small chapel where services were held every day.

1958

School opens

In January, the new Girls' Grammar School was at last opened on the corner of East Hill and Old Woking Road. The two-storey building would accommodate 540 girls and there would be ninety new pupils each year divided equally into three classes. As well as the spacious main hall, there were six laboratories, two domestic-science rooms with a self-contained flat, two art rooms, a soundproof music room and even a flat sunroof on which open-air classes could be held. The playing fields adjoined the school so the girls would no longer have to trudge from one end of the town to the other for games lessons.

The senior girls went in a day early for the purposes of orientation and the following day they helped the rest of the pupils to find their way around the new building.

For Eric's benefit

At the end of June a benefit cricket match for Eric Bedser was held at Horsell recreation ground in Brewery Road. Horsell Cricket Club played against a selection of Surrey cricketers. Eric Bedser had first played at the ground twenty-six years before. On this occasion Peter Edmunds of the home team hit several balls from the county player into Brewery Road for six.

Young love

Roger Wilson (22), a garage mechanic from Brookwood, and Mary Cary (17), a factory worker from Knaphill, wanted to get married. They had been going out together for six months but Mary's parents felt she was too young and did not know her own mind. As she was under eighteen, her father's permission was necessary.

However, the couple were so much in love they decided to take matters into their own hands. One morning, instead of going to work, they set off in Roger's van for Gretna Green where they could get married without the permission of Mary's father. Mr Cary reported his daughter missing but the police did not catch up with them until they had crossed the Scottish border. They stayed there for three weeks to fulfil the qualifying period and were then married. After the ceremony, they drove for over fourteen hours back to Woking, now legally married. Mrs Cary was disappointed that her daughter had not waited and been married in church but she and her husband accepted the marriage and were glad the couple planned to make their home in Woking.

Lest we forget

In October the Queen travelled to Brookwood to unveil the memorial commemorating the 3,500 men and women of the Commonwealth who had given their lives for the cause of freedom during the second world war. The memorial had been designed by the architect, Ralph Hobday. The names were inscribed on green slate panels and the Queen was presented with a register of the memorial. With her were the Queen Mother and the Duke of Gloucester, who was president of the Imperial War Graves Commission.

A crowd of 7,000 watched the unveiling and heard the Queen say, 'In this garden the memorial will be kept ever green.' She laid a wreath of roses and carnations. Other wreaths were then laid by the next of kin, many of whom wore black.

1959

Misty's bid for freedom

In January, Misty, a young horse belonging to Mrs Davison from Normandy, near Guildford, decided to do some exploring. It escaped from its paddock and headed for Brookwood where it was caught by police and held at Pirbright camp. But Misty had not seen enough. It broke its bonds and rushed across the road to where a football match was in progress. The terrified players scattered as it hurtled across the pitch. It then decided to head for London and made for the railway track. It galloped through Woking and the police sent a hurried signal to warn the driver of a fast rain from Waterloo that a horse was heading in his direction.

The noise of the approaching train frightened the animal so much that it turned round and headed back to Woking – towards a train travelling *to* Waterloo. Another signal was hurriedly dispatched. Bewildered by the noise, the trembling animal stopped in the middle of the track. A brave porter, James Ronald, approached it with a chain; eventually he was able, with difficulty, to coax it off the track and allow the trains to resume their interrupted journeys. Misty was taken to a nearby stable to await her distraught owner.

Gordon gets around

Also in January, across the other side of the world in Sudan, there was a coup d'etat. For the past fifty-four years, a statue of General Gordon, seated on a camel, had stood in Gordon Avenue, Khartoum. It had been designed by Onslow Ford and in 1902 it had been erected in London. In 1904 it was sent to Khartoum where it remained until the new regime decided that its rightful place was in England. The Foreign Office decided that the statue should be erected in the grounds of Gordon's Boys' School as the school had been founded in the general's memory. A picture of it in Khartoum, taken by Dr Bloss, a Woking resident, already hung in one of the classrooms.

It was not until April that the statue arrived in England having survived the long sea voyage on the troopship *Fort Dunvegan*. It made its journey to Gordon's Boys' School on a low-loader lorry and, when it arrived, it remained crated until a suitable site could be found.

Monty's leeks

In March, Field Marshal Viscount Montgomery visited Pirbright camp to present leeks to the officers of the first battalion Welsh Guards on the occasion of St David's day. The custom had originated in 1915.

Queen Mum at Ockenden

In May the Queen Mother paid an informal visit to Ockenden where she was shown round by Joyce Pearce and the chairman, Dr Christopher Woodward. The five girls who had been the first to be brought to Ockenden were presented to her. Then some of the girls, dressed in national costume, performed traditional songs and dances.

Chris Chataway MP

Chris Chataway left Woking to become the Conservative MP for North Lewisham; he was later made Post Office minister. Previously he had been a brewery executive and a television commentator.

1960

Fire!

One Monday at the beginning of January a bottle of spirit lacquer exploded at the rear of Michael Andrew's hairdressing salon in Walton Road. The surrounding area then caught fire and spread to the salon, causing panic. Women in curlers shot out from under hairdryers and rushed out of the building to take sanctuary in nearby shops. Fortunately no one was hurt and the fire brigade arrived promptly to douse the flames. The customers returned to their interrupted appointments to discover it was business as usual and that little damage had been done.

New post office opened

On 6 April the new post office was officially opened by Mr Stanley Higgins, chairman of Woking Council. It was situated on the site of the old council offices in Commercial Road. Mr Higgins made the first purchase and at two o'clock the post office was open for business to the public.

Gordon's statue

After remaining in its crate for several months, the statue of General Gordon, seated on a camel, was at last re-erected in the grounds of the Gordon's Boys' School. On 14 May it was unveiled by Lady Huddleston, the widow of a former governor general of the Sudan. The plinth on which it stood was designed and constructed by the Necropolis Company of Brookwood and was donated by Lady Huddleston in memory of her husband. On it was inscribed:

> Charles George Gordon born Woolwich 28 January 1833, killed Khartoum 26 January 1885. This statue was erected at Khartoum in 1904, removed and presented to the school in 1959. The plinth has been presented in memory of General Sir Hubert J. Huddleston who served in the Sudan for 24 years and was Governor General 1940–47.

The school mounted a guard of honour, which was inspected by Lord Rugby who was also a former governor of the Sudan. He was accompanied by the chairman of the governors, Admiral Sir John Edelsten, and the commandant, Brigadier Nottingham. Lord Rugby had been seven at the time of Gordon's murder and he remembered his mother telling him about it.

First woman chairman

On Tuesday 23 May the first woman chairman of Woking Council was elected unanimously. She was Mrs Dorothy Gale and she had been the Conservative member for St John's since 1954.

Dismissed

Sam Rendall from the Gambia, who lived in St John's, taught at West Byfleet County Secondary School. He was a good teacher but he fell in love with another member of staff and they started an affair. After it was discovered, it was obvious they could not remain at the school. When the headmaster, Mr Goodger, told them this, the woman immediately agreed to resign but Sam Rendall asked for time to think it over.

The next morning he was found dead in his classroom. He had electrocuted himself. Apparently he had been having psychological problems and was particularly concerned about a painful scar on his neck, which was the result of a particular tribal custom in his native country. At the inquest the coroner recorded a verdict of 'suicide while the balance of his mind was disturbed'.

Never too old

Although Alec Bedser had given up test cricket, and was now forty-two, he still played for Surrey. In his final game for the county he took five wickets for twenty-one, in twenty-one overs.

His playing career over, he managed the England cricket team during two overseas tours and then became an England selector for a number of years. He was eventually appointed chairman and held that post for thirteen years.

Woman cabbie

In November, for the first time, a woman joined the ranks of taxi drivers at Woking station. She was Miss Pat Walton and her arrival caused consternation among some of the male drivers.

1961

Emigration at eighty

Since their marriage in 1912 at St Paul's Church, Maybury, Mr and Mrs Henry Hill had lived in the same house in Princess Road for forty-eight years. They had met when the groom had lodged with his bride's parents after leaving the Navy. The couple had been driven to their wedding in a horse-drawn carriage. Mrs Hill had lived in Maybury since she was four but her husband had seen more of the world during his time in the Navy.

In the 1950s their younger daughter, Dorothy, married and emigrated to Australia. She invited her parents to visit. Mr Hill had just retired and there seemed little to hold them in Woking. Having discussed it, they decided to follow their daughter's example. Mr Hill (80) and his wife (72) emigrated to Australia, proving that it is never too late to start a new life.

Berlin Wall

A 19-year-old student, Colin Williams of Ashwood Road, Woking, was in Berlin when the infamous wall was built. When he arrived in the city on 9 August, he found it 'happy, peaceful and calm'. Two days' later there was turmoil as barbed wire cut off the east of the city from the west and armed soldiers replaced the civilian police at the Brandenburg Gate. West Berlin demonstrated against the constriction of freedom but to no avail.

Williams and an American friend pretended to be journalists and entered East Berlin. The Woking man took photographs of tanks and armoured cars near the Brandenburg Gate; the soldiers guarding the roads with fixed bayonets were only boys of sixteen or seventeen. When a fire started at Humbolt University, he watched the building burn. Suddenly he was grabbed by five policemen brandishing rifles; he and his friend were hustled into a police truck and driven to police headquarters. At first he had thought the situation 'incredibly funny' but when all their possessions, including their passports, were confiscated, he realised it was serious. That night their meal consisted of dry bread and a sausage.

They were held for ten hours before being released. Colin Williams said later that he thought they had been arrested because of the fire. As they were not charged with arson, he assumed that the real culprits had been found. He was very glad to be free although their car had been ransacked. Fortunately, their other possessions, including their passports, had been returned and he had historic photographs to illustrate his experience.

Jeweller's burgled

Russell's, the jeweller's, was broken into one evening at the beginning of October and items worth over £3,000 were stolen. The theft was not discovered until the following morning when the assistants arrived to open the premises. Since the shop opened in 1908, there had only been one other burglary. That was in 1919 when goods valued at over £2,000 had been taken.

Special postmark

On 28 October the Post Office issued Woking with a special canceller for letters posted on that day. It was a great privilege as only a limited number of these were issued each year for special occasions.

The 'special occasion' on this day was the third annual convention of the Surrey Philatelic Society, which was to be held in Woking; all letters posted in the special pillar box in the convention hall would have a picture of the Shah Jehan Mosque stamped on to the envelope instead of the customary wavy lines.

Death of a pianist

Countess Adelina de Lara had lived in Woking for the past thirty years. She was a world-famous concert-pianist and had been the last of Clara Schumann's pupils to perform in public. She gave her first performance in Liverpool when she was only six and continued playing in public until she was in her eighties.

She died in the Victoria Hospital on 25 November after a short illness. The funeral service, held at Woking crematorium, was led by Michael Brettell, vicar of St Mary of Bethany.

'Contessa' opened

In December a radio personality opened a new Contessa underwear shop in Chertsey Road. She was Mrs Dorothy Lane who was a character in the popular *Mrs Dale's Diary* radio serial. Greeted by Mr Wilkie, managing director of Contessa's twenty-three shops, she cut the blue silk ribbon in front of the door. Describing the shop as 'up-to-date' and 'go-ahead', she then purchased a pair of stockings saying that she had laddered hers on the journey to Woking.

1962

Mercy flight

Flight Lieutenant Frederick Weaver, who lived in Wheatsheaf Close, was the grandson of Mr Quartermaine who had been chairman of Woking Council. Educated at Woking Grammar, Weaver had been a member of Woking School's Air Training Corps squadron.

In January he captained a four-engine Shackleton of Coastal Command on a mercy mission over the Atlantic. A 20-year-old sailor called Frederikson – a cook on board the Swedish shop SS *Portland* – was suffering from tetanus. Flight Lieutenant Weaver was based in Cornwall and at one o'clock in the morning he took off and headed for the Atlantic, carrying on board the necessary drugs for the sick man. Two hours later, with the help of a full moon, he was able to identify the ship beneath him and dropped the container on to the deck from a height of 250 feet.

Commemorating a hero

1962 was the seventy-sixth anniversary of the death of General Gordon. Seventy-year-old Mr Saunders, who had been a pupil at the school over fifty years ago, laid a wreath at the foot of the statue at a special ceremony. The boys had formed ranks around the statue and a wreath was laid on behalf of the school by Sergeant Spencer, the head boy. The chaplain, Reverend Giles, then led in prayer 'giving humble yet hearty thanks for the life and example of General Charles Gordon in whose memory this school was founded'.

Defence exercise

In March the Woking Civil Defence Unit held an exercise in Woking Park. The local Sea and Army Cadets acted as victims and the 'make up' was done by the first-aid section of the unit. The 'wounds' were so realistic that one elderly lady fainted when she saw a boy hobbling down the street with a jagged bone sticking out of his leg.

The exercise was successful apart from a minor incident when a brick fell on a Mr Oldfield who was in charge of rescuing 'casualties' from the second floor of a building. Fortunately, he was not hurt.

A new athletic ground

In May the Woking athletic ground was opened by Lieutenant-Colonel Wells, chairman of Surrey County Council. The project had taken about ten years to complete and had cost £26,000. Following the official opening, the first athletics match was held with Woking coming second out of five competitors.

Painting prize

In the National Schools' Painting Competition, 13-year-old Frida Naish of Sheerwater won a major prize in her age group. Her prize was a gold watch but she was also given a £20 cheque for her school and a framed print of a Van Gogh painting that would hang in the school.

1963

A bomb in the loft

Mr Holly, a partner in a Woking firm of chartered surveyors and accountants, had a shock when he went into the loft above his offices in Commercial Road. Tucked behind the rafters was a long, oval-shaped object. Mr Holly went closer. It couldn't be – could it? It was! It was definitely a bomb.

Mr Holly hurtled down the steps and rushed across to the phone. Officers from the police and the bomb-disposal squad arrived promptly and, having cleared the area, the bomb-disposal officer ascended the steps and gingerly approached the bomb. Then he grinned. It *was* a bomb but a fake one used for practice. He wondered how it had found its way into the offices of a respectable Woking firm.

Trinity Methodist sold

In March, Trinity Methodists sold the church in which they had worshipped for fifty-eight years. The buyer was the Norwich Union Life Insurance

Society. It was planned to build a new church in Brewery Road. It would seat 350 people – fewer than the old church, but there would be a number of ancillary buildings, which had been lacking in the previous accommodation.

The Stones in Atalanta

On 19 August the Rolling Stones performed a gig in the famous Atalanta ballroom. It was a night to remember. The pale-pink Atalanta had one of the best-sprung dance floors in the south-east and was a popular rendezvous for dances, concerts and discos. It had a resident band and was also in use during the day.

As well as the Rolling Stones, it had been visited by other bands and entertainers. On one occasion Dr Who and the Daleks caused shivers of terror up the spines of the audience of children who sat waiting for their town to be destroyed.

Christian aid

Fifty-year-old Sidney Dovan had originally been head waiter at the Talbot Hotel in Ripley, where he had earned £20 a week. Then things went wrong; he lost his job and he and his family were evicted by court order from their house in Ripley. Sidney did not treat the court with respect and had to serve a month in Brixton prison for contempt.

His wife and children deserted him and, after he left prison, he returned to Ripley and wandered the streets. The vicar of St Mary's Church, George Street, took pity on him and persuaded his parishioners to show Christian charity by feeding him. He also provided Sidney with accommodation – in the church.

He was given a plastic sheet on which to sleep in front of the altar. Every night at ten he entered the warm church where he slept until nine the next morning. Sundays were different. On those days he had to get up earlier because there was a service at eight o'clock. He attended all the services before curling up for another peaceful night's sleep in front of the altar.

Watkinson resigns

Harold Watkinson, MP for Woking, announced in April that he would not be standing at the next general election due to business commitments.

The amorous bull

Billy the bull, of Send Court farm, gazed wistfully across the river Wey. Then his eyes lit up. Surely that was a herd of cows on the other side of the river.

He would visit them; he was feeling amorous. Panting, he plunged into the water and started to wade across. Then disaster struck and he realised he was stuck fast in the mud.

Watchers on the bank called the fire brigade but, by the time they arrived, Billy had recovered his balance and reached the other shore. But 'all that glisters is not gold'. The herd he had struggled to reach were steers – not cows. To complete his humiliation, he had to trudge six miles home along the road to reach his farm. He was exhausted when he finally arrived. It had been a very frustrating day.

Labour chairman

In May, Mrs Rhoda McGaw was elected chairman of Woking Council. The previous chairman, Marjorie Richardson, automatically became vice-chairman so, for the first time, two women headed the council. It was also the first time that Woking had had a Labour chairman. Mrs McGaw had been the member for the central ward for the past eight years.

1964

Joyce Pearce OBE

In the New Year's Honours List, Joyce Pearce, the founder of the Ockenden Venture, received an OBE.

Fab four

The Beatles paid a visit to Woking in January. The winners of a competition run by the YMCA were to meet the famous quartet. The competition was won by David Coltart and Marilyn Etherington and, when the Beatles arrived, each member of the group was enrolled as a member of the YMCA.

Striking gold

In February, for the first time, a Woking resident won a gold medal in the Winter Olympics. He was Captain Robin Dixon, the son of Lord Glentoren and he lived in Heathside Road. A parachutist with the Grenadier Guards, Dixon was stationed at Pirbright and trained in Switzerland for the two-man bobsleigh event in Innsbruck.

He and his partner, Tony Nash, were delighted to win this event and receive gold medals. Later they were both feted at a civic reception in Christ Church hall, which was transformed for the evening into a sports arena. About four hundred local sportsmen and women attended and the chairman of the Woking Council, Mrs McGaw, paid tribute to their achievement.

Afterwards Dixon showed some slides of bobsleighing and talked about his experiences before signing his name for young autograph hunters.

Lifesaver

At only nine years of age, Jane Gray of East Hill, Maybury, won the Royal Lifesaving Society's intermediate lifesaving award – perhaps the youngest person to have done so.

Trinity Methodist

At the end of March a wooden cross was erected on the site of the new Methodist church in Brewery Road and a dedication service was held. In May the foundation stone was laid by three generations of worshippers. The silver trowel had also been used on several occasions by members of the royal family.

The engraving on the stone was done by Mrs Gillian Maddison who had been evacuated to Woking during the war; she had fond memories of Trinity Methodist church, which she had attended. The words on the stone read: 'To the glory of God this stone was laid on 23 May 1964 with thanksgiving for the erection of this church which replaces those which stood in Church Street from 1871 and in Commercial Road from 1905. Other foundations can no man lay than that which is laid which is Jesus Christ.'

Princess Anne's High Jinks

In April Princess Anne attended the Hunter Trials and Show Jumping at Chobham. On her pony, High Jinks, she won a prize in the junior pairs event; she had a clear round in the showjumping but was not placed.

Ball of fire

Friday, 12 June saw the worst storm ever experienced in the Woking area. Torrential rain was accompanied by deafening thunder and forked lightning; a house in Heathside Road was struck by lightning causing a great deal of damage but no casualties. All the lights were out for over an hour.

A group of Woking people returning home on a coach trip from London had the most frightening time. They were crawling along Old Woking Road because the driver was finding it difficult to see through the rain. Suddenly there was a loud bang and lightning flashed in front of the coach.

Looking out of the nearside windows, the terrified passengers saw a huge ball of fire rolling along beside them while an unpleasant odour permeated the coach. Fortunately the fireball kept its distance and they arrived home safely but it was an experience none of them was likely to forget.

1965

End of an era

Inkerman Barracks had been home to soldiers for over a century. For the past twenty years it had been occupied by the Royal Military Police. The barracks closed in February and the Redcaps moved to new barracks in Chichester. A new secondary school was to be built on the site.

Tenth anniversary

Ockenden Venture celebrated its tenth anniversary. It now had sixteen homes in England and Wales and had helped 600 children. In July movie star Ingrid Bergman paid a visit. She had been very interested in the plight of refugee children since she had played the part of Gladys Aylward in the film *The Inn of the Sixth Happiness*.

Modest artist

Lieutenant-Colonel Claude Rowberry lived in Lavender Road, Maybury for the last ten years of his life. Three years after his death, his son opened a padlocked steel trunk that his father had left him. Inside, he discovered paintings and drawings in a variety of styles and using various techniques. He knew that his father had always painted obsessively but no one had ever seen his paintings.

However, on his death bed, he had said to his son, 'When I'm gone, try to do something about my paintings.'

The paintings were eventually shown to experts who agreed that this modest artist had real talent and his work should be displayed so that others could appreciate it. The paintings were exhibited in the Daedalus Gallery in Chertsey; the curator was excited about the find.

Rowberry had served in a cavalry regiment during the first world war and had been mentioned in dispatches. In Flanders, for the first time, he was suddenly seized with the desire to paint as he gazed at the 'terrible beauty of the battlefield'. Although often in danger, he produced a great number of paintings from the front line. Returning home, all his paintings were hidden from view in the locked trunk.

During the second world war, he was stationed in England; in his helmet and colonel's uniform he sat at his easel surrounded by burning buildings while hurriedly recording the London blitz for posterity. No efforts by the emergency services could move him; he was not afraid of danger but was terrified of anyone seeing his work. All these paintings eventually joined the others in the trunk. It was not until after his death that others could appreciate what this dedicated artist had achieved.

Sheerwater success

Six Sheerwater pupils achieved fame in September when they became finalists in the television programme *Stubby's Silver Star Show*. Calling themselves The Trebles, four boys played guitars and drums and they had two vocalists – a boy and a girl. The youngest was Lynne Harrison who was only twelve.

Thirteen-year-old Colin Wick from the same school also did well. He was given a part in Lionel Bart's musical, *Maggie May*. He had already had small parts on television and in the West End.

Send for May

In November Flight Lieutenant May, who had lived all his life in Send, went to Buckingham Palace to receive his MBE from the Queen; she chatted to him about his work with young people.

He was a commander of the Brooklands squadron and also of the Send 'Flight of the Air Training Corps'. He had recently retired but remained active.

Bomb blast

The year ended with a bang. Just before Christmas a home-made bomb was planted in the garden below a window of the chamber in the Woking Council offices. It exploded just after eleven o'clock at night but no one called the police. Nearby residents, who heard the explosion, assumed it was a car backfiring so the damage was not discovered until the following morning.

The shattered window had shed glass all over the lawn and the council chamber was scarred from the blast. The perpetrator was never found and fortunately no one was injured.

1966

Ingrid's appeal

On 6 February Ingrid Bergman appeared on the television show *Be so Kind* to appeal on behalf of the Ockenden Venture. The script was written in accordance with the star's own ideas. She described the Ockenden Venture as 'a unique movement which sets out to give a home and education to young refugees of every race, colour and creed'.

New art gallery

Alwyn Crawshaw, a commercial artist, had lived in Woking for fourteen years and was determined 'to stimulate art in the town'. To this end, he opened an art gallery in Commercial Road in which local artists could exhibit their paintings. Called, not surprisingly, the Crawshaw Gallery, it was staffed by his sister, Pamela; another sister, Shirley, and the artist's wife, June, exhibited their work while one area was devoted entirely to Alwyn Crawshaw's own work.

Fire-fighting nuns

In March a fire started on the roof of St Peter's Anglican convalescent home in Maybury. Black-robed nuns from the adjacent convent fought the blaze until the fire brigade arrived. Patients were helped from their beds to safety but the nuns needed the firemen to help them after the fire was out as the lift was not working. Fortunately there was not too much damage and no one was hurt.

Success for Frank

Frank Summerscale had always wanted to act. Since he was twelve, he had had small parts in television commercials. After he left Goldsworth County Secondary School, he changed his name to Frank Somers and landed the part of Curley, one of the 'lost boys' in a London production of *Peter Pan*, which then went on tour. In May 1966 he was thrilled to be offered a part in the musical *Camelot* and hoped this would lead to even greater things.

Bambi goes walkabout

Bambi, a three-foot-tall deer, decided to go for a walk. On Whit Monday, she explored the gardens in Oriental Road and Pembroke Road, leaping over the fences that divided them. She was too fast for the residents to catch and a police motorcyclist went in search of her but he had no success either. Then she wandered into the grounds of Wynberg, an old people's home, in Oriental Road and entertained the old folk by leaping gracefully into a rhododendron bush before heading for the nearby woods closely pursued by the warden of the home, Thomas Sullivan. But she disappeared and was not seen in the Woking area again. Perhaps she had found her way back to Milford or Cranleigh where there was a herd of deer and from where she might have originated.

Destroyed by fire

In the early morning of 3 December the fire brigade received an urgent call. The seventeenth century Newark Mill near Ripley was on fire. The blaze was fierce but in spite of the sterling efforts of both the Woking and Guildford fire services, the mill could not be saved. All that remained of the five-storey wooden building were twisted pieces of metal and old grinding stones. A huge area around the building had also been devastated but fortunately there had been no one around so no one was hurt. Because of the extensive damage, the police were not able to identify the cause of the fire but the wooden structure had always been a fire hazard; there seemed to be no evidence of arson.

There had been a mill on the site since Anglo-Saxon times and it was referred to in the Domesday Book of 1086 as 'a mill which pays 21*s*. 6*d*.' What happened to the earlier mill is not known but the one that met its sad end in December was probably built in the middle of the seventeenth century. It had the distinction of claiming to be the oldest mill in the county and was one of Surrey's best known landmarks.

1967

Invasion force

In October Woking was startled to witness the unusual sight of the army marching through the town in full battledress. No, England was not at war again! It was a recruitment drive to encourage young men to join the Queen's Regiment, which had recently returned from four years' service in West Germany.

The parade was led by a military band, followed by 160 soldiers of all ranks. They marched from Knaphill, along Goldsworth Road, through the town and came to a halt in Sheerwater. Here, they rested on the grass verges while they ate a leisurely lunch before continuing their march to West Byfleet.

Some of the soldiers were from Woking; one of them, Michael Cranfield, lived in Albert Drive so he left his companions and went to have lunch with his parents.

Their big fat Greek wedding

Rosemary McBirney and Antony Michaelides left their Woking wedding reception richer than they had entered it. As they danced in the banqueting room of Mr Homer Michaelides's restaurant, the guests pinned £1 and £5 notes to their clothes. The bridegroom, an accountant from Woking, was of Greek extraction and the couple had earlier been married in a Greek Orthodox Church in Shepherds Bush. It is a Greek custom to pin money to the bridal pair to give them a good start in life.

The bride was from Newcastle but she was destined to travel even further away from her roots as the couple planned to emigrate to Australia.

Breathalyser blues

The new breathalyser law angered publicans because much of their trade came from car drivers, many of whom were now avoiding pubs.

When Barbara Castle, the transport minister, arrived in Hookheath to open an extension to the British Transport staff college, she was greeted by twenty-four angry landlords waving placards at her. In spite of the jeers – one placard read 'Three Boos for Barbs' – Mrs Castle was unmoved and continued with her visit. The countrywide protests had no effect; the breathalyser was here to stay.

Peter Robinson, the licensee of the Robin Hood Inn in Knaphill, decided to do something positive to attract his lost customers. For four nights a week he ran a door-to-door minibus service so that his customers could drink without having to drive home. Punters were so delighted with the scheme that they insisted on paying for the service although the landlord had planned to offer it free.

Attacked by a donkey

Three-year-old Robin Clarke wandered into the grounds of Southbrook in Chobham while his mother was visiting the house. In the paddock he saw a donkey and climbed in to get closer to it. He had often fed it carrots with his mother. But the animal objected to its territory being invaded and attacked the child. When Mrs Clarke missed her son, she was frantic and eventually discovered him lying unconscious in the paddock with broken ribs and deep gashes on his face. The donkey, standing nearby, was unconcerned.

Robin was rushed to hospital and for three days surgeons fought to save his life. Fortunately they were successful and the invalid was later allowed home with all his body parts functioning correctly.

Clementine's delight

The new secondary school in Knaphill, which had been built on the site of Inkerman Barracks, had been open for a year and had 600 pupils but it had not been officially opened and there had been some discussion about its name. Many pupils wanted it to be called after Winston Churchill. One pupil, Michael Schofield, even wrote to Lady Clementine Churchill asking for permission to use her husband's name. She replied in the affirmative and perhaps this was the deciding factor in the choice of the name – Winston Churchill County Secondary School. A picture of the great man was placed in the entrance.

At the end of November, Lady Churchill travelled to Woking to perform the opening ceremony, which was presided over by Irvine Smith, chairman of the Surrey education committee. She and other important guests were welcomed by Mr Gibson, chairman of Woking Urban District Council.

Royal Crown

Lyn Crown, a former Sheerwater pupil, came top in her City and Guilds cookery examination, specialising in French cuisine. She decided to gain more experience and applied to work in the royal kitchen at Windsor. She was delighted to be accepted and spent her Christmas preparing meals in the huge royal kitchen for the Queen and her guests. However, she had to concentrate on her own job and never saw a complete meal. Neither was she able to make use of her speciality as the Queen prefers simple food with no trimmings.

1968

Pigs on the prowl

Mrs Joy Rutter was the smallholder of Sandlewood goat farm, which was next to the Barnsbury estate off Goldsworth Road. She also owned a herd of pigs that were not happy at sharing their accommodation with the goats. One evening they went on the rampage around the estate. They dug up lawns, ripped down hedges, tore up the flower beds and ate the vegetables. The residents were furious and petitioned the council for protection from the marauding herd. But the council was not interested and said it was the farmer's responsibility to keep her animals under control. Mrs Rutter was *not* a popular lady.

Albion House opened

In April, Ivor Gibson, chairman of Woking Council, opened Albion House on the site of the Albion Hotel, which had been demolished in 1965. At eight storeys, it was the tallest building in Woking. The ground floor contained thirteen shops and three flats and the other floors consisted of offices.

Mother-of-three murdered

On 24 July, Kathy Ives – who had just given birth to her third child – was found badly beaten in her bedroom at Sutton Green. The attack had been so vicious that blood had even splattered on the ceiling. Her three small children were in the house with her.

She was found by a Mr Ryder who kept his Dormobile at the Ives' house. Thinking it strange that no children were playing in the garden, he knocked at the door which was opened by 4-year-old Vivienne. When he went into the bedroom, he found Mrs Ives lying in a pool of blood, but still alive. She died that afternoon in the Royal Surrey County Hospital in Guildford. After the birth of her first child, Kathy Ives had suffered from mental illness and had been in Brookwood Hospital for some time but she seemed to have recovered and had no trouble after the birth of her two other children.

Harold Ives was told of the attack on his wife and identified her by her rings. Later he made a long statement to the police telling them of his two-year affair with Pat, a 17-year-old schoolgirl. On the day he had taken his wife home from hospital, he had had sex with Pat who didn't know his wife had just had a baby.

On the morning of the murder he said that Kathy had been 'ranting and raving' at him. She said she was going to 'get rid of the kids' and he was afraid for their safety. He hit his wife to 'stop her mumbling'. He assured the police that she had been alive when he left. The key of the house, which he had locked, and the axe, the murder weapon, were later found in Knaphill.

Harold Frederick Ives was charged with murdering his wife and in December stood trial at Lewes. He was found guilty and jailed for life.

Fire at Robinson's

One Saturday evening just before Christmas a fire broke out in the kitchen at Robinson's department store in Chertsey Road. It was not discovered until early the next morning when smoke could be seen billowing around the building. Apart from the damage to the restaurant, the rest of the floors suffered only smoke damage; plans for the Christmas period were not affected but the repairs to the restaurant would take three months to complete.

1969

Out of the frying pan

Stanislaw Rasek and Peter Schwab escaped from Czechoslovakia after the invasion of their country. They thought they had found safety in England. However, at the end of September, they were caught in an explosion at the Metalising factory in Monument Way East. They were working in the metal-spraying section when something near the propane-gas equipment exploded and they were engulfed in flames. Both were badly burned and rushed to Roehampton hospital where they were eventually said to be in 'a satisfactory condition' although they would always carry the scars of their ordeal.

Illegal immigrant

Mr Mohammed Saleen from Pakistan was arrested on 25 November after a police raid on his house in Maybury. He had been working at the Sorbo works in Sheerwater, but was an illegal immigrant. He had been given the job after producing a forged card.

He told the police through an Urdu interpreter that he had wanted to come to Britain to get a better education, but the British High Commission had turned down his application. So he decided to ignore official channels. He borrowed money to pay for a false passport and airline tickets. He flew to Rawalpindi and then on to France. Here, with other Muslims, Sikhs and Hindus, he was loaded into a boat and eventually decanted on to English soil.

Once in England, arrangements were made for him to travel to Woking without being seen by any customs officials. He told the Woking court, 'I hope the British Government will be kind to me, to keep me and make my future bright.' He was remanded in custody until the New Year.

Teachers' strike

On 26 November fifty Woking teachers paraded through the town bearing placards protesting against their 'unrealistic' pay offer. They marched from the council offices to Christ Church hall. It was the first time teachers had gone on strike and their decision had not been taken lightly. The strike had been called by the Woking and District Teachers' Association, the local branch of the National Union of Teachers. It was part of the national campaign to improve their pay. Young teachers found it very difficult to live on their salaries. The campaign was supported by the local MP, Cranley Onslow, who said they had a 'strong case' and had already signed a parliamentary motion in their favour.

1970

Visit to St James

Mrs Mockett, a sister tutor at the Woking Victoria Hospital, was a member of the board of assessors for the General Nursing Council. 1970 was the golden jubilee of the council and Mrs Mockett was one of the five hundred guests invited to St James' Palace to meet the Queen Mother. With her, went her husband and Dr Nan Dakumar, the senior surgical-house-officer at the same hospital. All the guests wore evening dress.

The Queen Mother, escorted by two corgis, was dressed in a black crinoline as she was in mourning for her son-in-law's mother, Princess Andrew of Greece. The throne room, where the presentation took place, was lavishly decorated in red and gold with priceless oil paintings hanging on the walls. The royal hostess chatted to Mrs Mockett about her work with students and also commented on articles the sister tutor had written.

Family reunited

Reverend and Mrs Egemba Igwe went to Ockenden and saw their four children for the first time for a month. The children had come to England from war-torn Biafra in December and were at school at Greenfield. When the war with Nigeria ended, their parents were at a conference in Ghana and so were able to escape to England to join their family.

Schoolboy star

Ian Weighill, a 13-year-old schoolboy from Sheerwater, enjoyed acting so much that he persuaded his mother to write to the Cambridge Manor stage school in Weybridge to ask for an audition. Mrs Hamilton, the principal, was very impressed and Ian was enrolled at the school.

As a result, he eventually auditioned for a part in the new Walt Disney film, *Bedknobs and Broomsticks*. To his delight he was chosen to play the role of

Charlie, a cockney evacuee, who resorts to blackmail to get money to provide a better life for himself and his siblings.

His mother said that the part fitted Ian – who was a true cockney – 'like a glove'. She would go to Hollywood with him as a chaperon for the three months he would have to stay there to make the film. The only question was: would he be able to settle back into life at Sheerwater school when he returned?

Bomb scare

Sheerwater School was in the news again one Monday morning at the end of March. An anonymous caller had informed the head that there was a bomb in the school. When the pupils arrived, they were not allowed to go into the building. They remained in the playground while the police and staff searched the school. Nothing was found and it was clear that a hoaxer had disrupted the school day.

Queen's Award for Industry

EFCO Ltd in Sheerwater won the Queen's Award for Industry because of its success with exports. It sold millions of pounds worth of electroplating and polishing machines and metal-treatment furnaces. Most of its orders were from Iron Curtain countries. The flag, denoting the factory's success, was raised outside the offices by Gilbert Williams who had been chauffeur to one of the founders of the company, the late Donald Campbell.

Butterfly guide

Dr Lionel Higgins, a gynaecologist, had always been interested in butterflies. He had started collecting them when he was seven and one room in his Chobham home was entirely taken over by his collection. When he retired, he decided to share his enthusiasm with others. With Norman Riley, the keeper of entomology at the British Museum, he wrote the first complete guide to British butterflies. As many of the species had become extinct, the book would be a valuable source for future entomologists.

Save the Atalanta

Twenty-seven-year-old Miss Sylvia Curtis had been going to the Atalanta ballroom every week since she was fourteen. She was very upset that the building was to be demolished and decided to organise a petition. She collected a thousand signatures and the petition, which was presented to the council on 18 December, covered several yards of paper. Sadly her efforts were in vain and the building was still scheduled for demolition.

1971

Achilles heel

In the 1960s a group of professional men in Woking were concerned that there was a lack of suitable housing for the elderly and they formed the Achilles Housing Society. There was no Greek connection. Apparently they wanted to be as near the beginning of the alphabet as possible!

However, when they contacted the Housing Corporation they were told that they had to be an 'Association' rather than a 'Society' and they could not use the name 'Achilles' again. As they still wished to use it, The *Second* Achilles Housing Association was formed in 1969. The chairman was Ken Turner, a solicitor, and the search was on for a suitable building that could be converted into flats for the elderly.

One was eventually found in Carlton Road. The owner of Woodham Place was delighted to sell it when he heard of the use to which his home was to be put. The housing association converted the original building into nine bedsits. Then an extension was built to house ten more purpose-built flats. Woodham Place was officially opened in 1971 by Mr Cranley Onslow.

Star plays truant

Ian Weighill – who had gone to Hollywood to play Charlie in *Bedknobs and Broomsticks* – found it difficult to settle down into the mundane life of school at Sheerwater when he returned from enjoying the high life in the film capital.

He played truant and, because both his mother and stepfather were at work all day, they assumed he was at school. They were horrified when they discovered that, between January and April, Ian had only attended school 26 times out of a possible 122.

They were summoned before Woking magistrates and pleaded guilty to letting their son play truant. However, they said that he had been ill when he had returned from America and was still receiving medical treatment. The magistrates adjourned the case for two months and Ian returned to school wearing a signet ring, which was promptly confiscated until the end of term. He still found it difficult to settle down.

A 'woman of the people'

On 5 July Mrs Rhoda McGaw, who lived in the Hockering, died at the Nuffield nursing home in Shores Road. She had been ill for some time. Known as 'a woman of the people' – although she had been educated privately – she read sociology at London University and became a member of the Labour Party. She was Woking Council's first Labour chairman and during her time on the council worked tirelessly for local people.

She was an atheist and the funeral was private but, at the end of July, a memorial meeting was held in the hall of St Andrew's Presbyterian Church. Many tributes were paid to her and the council promised to discuss a fitting memorial.

Burnt alive

In 1954 Kenneth Reynolds had had a serious accident when his motorbike collided with a petrol tanker. He was left a 'charred wreck' and spent three years in hospital being treated, not only for his physical injuries but also for mental illness. He worked as a carpenter in Mayford and was relieved when he was eventually able to return to work. However, he was upset to discover that his pay had been halved. He continued to suffer from depression and attempted suicide on three occasions.

On 28 July 1971 his fourth suicide attempt was successful. Carrying some matches, he went out into his garden, doused himself with petrol and burned himself to death. He was discovered lying on a patch of scorched grass surrounded by charred deckchairs. The only part of him not burnt were the cuffs of his trousers and his shoes. At the inquest, the coroner described it as 'a tragic case'.

In the stocks

Neal Cheeseman and Michael Cardy had to undergo a closing ritual at the end of their five-year apprenticeship at Unwin's the printers in Old Woking. Known as 'banging out', it was something every apprentice had to suffer at the end of his training.

A revolting mixture of sour milk, beer and treacle had been fermenting for three weeks previously. This was hurled over the unlucky young men by their colleagues and they were then flung into a mill pond. As if that wasn't enough, they were then put in the stocks while friends threw rotten eggs and tomatoes at them. By the end of their ordeal, they were relieved to go home and soak off the unpleasant mixture in hot baths. They described it as 'great fun' but were glad they were not scheduled for a repeat performance.

Foundation laid

On Monday, 18 October, Mr David Boorman, chairman of Woking Council, laid the foundation stone of the new shopping centre on a low brick wall near Christ Church. A set of the new decimal coins had been placed below the stone.

1972

Tragic death

David Harrison, a building worker from Sheerwater, was crushed to death when tons of concrete collapsed above him and crashed to the ground. He was working on a new office block on Pyrford Road. Firemen who rushed to the scene tried to dig him out with their bare hands but it was too late. He was the only fatality but others were seriously injured.

Curtains for Atalanta

At the end of January, the demolition gang finally moved in on the Atalanta ballroom. The building had originally been a Methodist manse and later it was the YMCA headquarters before it became the popular ballroom.

Power cuts

Woking residents, like the rest of the country, were unhappy with the frequent power cuts. However, they became angry when they discovered all the street lights blazing during the day. They demanded to know why the council was wasting electricity in this way when most people were suffering from a lack of heating and lighting.

The electricity board tried to calm the situation by pointing out that power cuts were implemented on a strict rota system so no one house had more than another. As for the street lights remaining on during the day, apparently they all had to be switched off manually and this took time. Residents were not impressed.

The heavens erupt

March saw one of the most violent thunderstorms ever experienced in Woking. Lightning struck a huge oak tree in Horsell causing balls of red fire to dance around Mary Cheshire's garden, billowing out clouds of red and yellow smoke. She had been watching television when the picture disintegrated into flashes and zigzags; then the house was plunged into darkness but, looking out of the window, she was treated to a private firework display. She thought at first the house had been struck by lightning but fortunately it was safe.

The next day the damage was assessed. In her garden, the shed door was broken, tools had been hurled around and soil had been thrown up on the roof. Apparently the lightning had struck the trunk of the oak tree, travelled down it and then moved on to melt the staples that attached it to the barbed wire. The force of the heat dented the earth forming a large crater. Fortunately no one was injured.

Alderton's local

In November John Alderton, the television actor, pulled a pint at his local, the Victoria in Woodham Lane. It was the first pint to be pulled after a £20,000 renovation of the pub.

1973

Miss Hill OBE

Miss Violet Hill, who had been the headmistress of the Girls' Grammar School since 1946, was awarded an OBE in the New Year honours' list. 1973 marked the golden jubilee of the school and Miss Hill retired at the end of the school year.

Council break-in

A very odd situation arose at the beginning of January. A sheriff's officer and Woking's deputy clerk, Mr Alfred Vice, stood by while a council workman smashed a pane of glass in Christ Church hall and put his hand through to open the side door so that the council could gain access.

The churchwarden, Brian Grout, rushed forward and offered a bunch of keys but it was too late. The council had already broken in. The church authorities were not happy about the methods used. They felt that a warrant should have been obtained and pointed out that they had not been asked to produce the keys before the forced entry. Most authorities would not consider doing this.

Negotiations between the church and the council had been going on for some time as the church-hall site was required for redevelopment. But the action taken was in breach of an undertaking signed in 1968 when the council promised to provide alternative accommodation for the church before taking possession of the site. A new hall was to be built but the council had not made provision for a choir vestry; the church did not wish to lose its original hall until the council had met its obligations in full.

A compromise was reached when a temporary hut was erected in the church grounds for the use of the choir. The sheriff's officer later told Peter

Searle, the vicar of Christ Church, that he was very sorry about what had happened.

Foundations laid

On 21 January, in pouring rain, Mr Harry Keat, chairman of Woking Council, laid the foundation stone of the new civic hall complex which would be known as Centre Halls. It was to include a small theatre with a seating capacity for about 250. This would be used for drama, films, lectures and concerts. There would also be a main hall, which would cater for about 750 people. For banquets it would comfortably seat 250. Rehearsal rooms, a restaurant, a bar and a club room would complete the new complex.

Achilles Place

In February, the Second Achilles Housing Association opened its second building. This was a purpose-built block of flats for the elderly in Bullbeggars Lane, Horsell. Named appropriately, Achilles Place, it was officially opened by Lady Howe, the wife of cabinet minister Sir Geoffrey Howe. Mr Ken Turner, the chairman of the housing association, presided at the ceremony.

Top dog

Mrs Butler of the Wey Farm, Ottershaw, was delighted when her Pembroke Welsh collie, Ch. Georgette of Wey, finished in the top six at Crufts. The collie won the Send gold vase for being top of her working group and was declared the fourth best in the show.

Jinxed painting?

Miss Molly Brett, who lived in Horsell, was an illustrator of children's books. Because she intended to change the décor of her living room, she decided to sell two paintings that had been owned by three generations of her family. Both were by the same artist; one was a self-portrait and the other was of an unidentified woman.

Miss Brett sold the paintings to Keith Mansfield of Barber's Antiques in Chertsey Road. He had them restored; the self-portrait was bought by a local man who wanted to hang it in an extension he had just built. Two days' later he returned the painting asking for his money back. It had brought bad luck to his family, he told Mr Mansfield. There had been three incidents. He had fallen downstairs, his wife had been injured and his children had fallen ill for no apparent reason. As he did not appear to be a superstitious type, the painting was taken back and placed next to the portrait of the woman, on the wall beside the staircase.

Three more incidents followed swiftly. Mr Mansfield tripped on the stairs, an expensive piece of porcelain was knocked off a table and, in the picture-framing department, John Murray dropped a sheet of glass. He had never done such a thing before. That was not all. A valuable piece of furniture was damaged by a removal man and finally the street door fell off its hinges!

Miss Brett, informed of the mishaps, said she knew of no previous bad luck associated with the painting. However, the subject of the second painting had once fallen downstairs and broken her leg but had then lived to the grand old age of ninety-four!

Death on Horsell Common

In March a student, walking on Horsell Common, made a gruesome discovery. A human skeleton, partly buried by moss, lay on the ground with old food containers nearby. It was wearing the remains of green cord-trousers, a white shirt and a quilted brown mackintosh.

A watch and a gold signet ring bearing the initials P. Y. helped his wife to identify him after a police appeal on television. He was Paul Tomlinson of Isleworth who had disappeared in April 1970. He had been the site foreman for a large building contractor and was studying for his surveyor's examinations. The P. Y. stood for the initials of his and his wife's first names.

The following month another body was found in a ditch on Horsell Common, near Littlewick Road. The deceased was also identified by his wife after another police appeal on television. He was James Williamson of Maybury, who worked for the British Aircraft Corporation in Weybridge.

Foul play was not suspected in either case.

1974

Followed by the KGB

Michael Scammell of St John's Road, Woking, spoke Russian fluently and was a frequent visitor to that country. He had many Russian friends including exiles in England. He was a Russian translator and had edited Solzhenitsyn's book *The Gulag Archipelago*.

However, when he went to Russia in January things were different. He was followed everywhere he went by the Soviet secret police. Because of this, he hid his notebook in a packet of tea although it only contained a list of books and some innocuous notes. Also in his pocket was a letter from the Russian actress, Lydia Chukouskaye; it was addressed to an exiled Russian physicist in Britain. Scammell had promised to post it for her when he returned home.

Unfortunately, he had forgotten about it and when he was searched, it was found and confiscated. Also confiscated was his notebook, which the KGB considered 'harmful to the interests of the Soviet Republic'. During his many visits to the country, he had never been searched although he was aware that *any* printed matter – even letters – had to be declared and he had not done this. Lydia Chukouskaye was not popular with the Soviet authorities and the discovery of her letter inevitably linked Michael with her. He assured the police that all his printed matter was innocent but they did not believe him and he was expelled. He felt that the KGB 'had made themselves a laughing stock' and given him plenty of publicity.

Present for a princess

Ten-year-old Anthony Garcia of Old Woking suffered from muscular dystrophy but that did not prevent him enjoying life. He was an enthusiastic member of the Disabled Riding Association, of which Princess Anne was patron.

Anthony's other interest was pottery and he made a pottery fruit bowl, which he had hand-painted for the Princess. It was a wedding gift for her and her groom, Captain Mark Philips. He took it to London hoping to be able to give it to her personally but he was not able to do so. However, he received an acknowledgement from her and an invitation to visit Buckingham Palace later in the year.

Seal of approval

1974 was an important year for Woking. After two failed attempts, the Urban District Council was at last successful in its attempt to obtain royal consent for elevating itself to the status of a borough council. To achieve this, all elected members of the council had to give their approval. One dissenting voice would have meant yet another refusal by the Queen. Fortunately there were no dissenting voices and Woking officially became a borough on 1 April.

The last chairman of the district council was David Robinson and it was he who had the privilege of collecting the royal charter parchment-scroll and seal from the Houses of Parliament. One side of the royal seal shows the Queen in Westminster Abbey and on the other side she is seen on horseback taking the salute in Horseguards Parade.

The first mayor of Woking *Borough* Council was Christopher Meredyth Mitchell, who was councillor for Horsell ward and lived in Hook Heath Road.

He was a director of a local company called Kennedy & Donkin. In recognition of his association with them, the company presented him with his mayoral robes made of fine scarlet cloth with fur trimming and underlined with white silk. Shoulder ribbons were added to hold the chain of office in place. An Irish lace jabot completed the outfit while for his head he was given a cocked hat sporting a golden loop. Future lady mayors would wear a tricorne hat. The robes were made by Ede & Ravencroft, robemakers and tailors to the royal family, and cost Kenny & Donkin £199. They would be worn on all civic occasions like church services and council meetings.

James Walker & Company, a local packing firm, presented the mayor with his gold badge of office, which bore the arms of Woking Borough Council; underneath this were the words *Fide et Dilegentia* (faithful and diligent). The chain of office was already in existence but would now be inscribed with the name of the *mayor* instead of the *chairman* of the council.

The royal mace, made by Shaw & Sons of London, was presented to the new borough by Mr Long, a director of the Norwich Union Insurance Company. It cost £1,480. Forty-four inches long, it was made of silver gilt. On ceremonial occasions the macebearer walks before the mayor. The head of the mace bearing Woking Borough's coat of arms faces the front, reminding the public that the mayor represents the people of Woking. The rear of the mace, depicting the royal coat of arms, faces the mayor as a reminder that he or she is the representative of the Queen.

In the past the mace was a weapon of war and was used in battle. Now, fortunately, it is only a symbol of authority.

1975

Angel of Peace moved

In February, two representatives of the British Legion watched as the Angel of Peace was hoisted off its base in Sparrow Park where it had rested for over fifty years. It was the first war memorial to be moved. It was taken to Grenville Martin's stonemason's yard in Church Street to be thoroughly cleaned before being moved to its new home.

On 21 April, the Queen's birthday, it was ceremonially hoisted into place in the Town Square above the stone column containing the names of those who had died in two world wars. The final ceremony was performed on 11 May. The war memorial was draped in the Union Jack and crowds watched as it was unveiled by Lord Hamilton, the Lord Lieutenant of Surrey. The service that followed was led by Peter Searle, vicar of Christ Church.

Hexagonal market

In April the new covered market at Victoria Arch was officially opened by the mayor. The unusual hexagonal design was reflected in the paving stones of the pedestrian section.

Closure

The Girls' Grammar School finally closed its doors at the end of the school year. In September it reopened as the Queen Elizabeth II comprehensive. In future it would be known as the QE2.

Bookworm

Brendan Stewart of Old Woking was a bookworm. He liked to find a quiet spot to enjoy his love of reading. His latest reading matter was *Swans at my Window* by Ginny Brown and he looked around for somewhere to enjoy it. He found it at the top of a fifty-foot electricity pylon in a field near Unwin's printing works. He climbed over a barbed-wire fence and scaled the pylon by putting his feet on the metal bolts attached to the sides.

When he reached the top, he settled down to read. It was a beautiful autumn day and, after reading for a while, he leant over to admire the view. That was a mistake! He accidentally touched a 'live' part of the pylon and 33,000 volts of electricity shot through him. He became a 'human battery' as sparks burst all around him, a flash exploded in his face, pain shot up his arm, his shirt sleeve was on fire and his hand was smoking.

Still clutching his book, he scrambled down the pylon and managed to stagger to a nearby pub, the Crown and Anchor, where he called for an ambulance. He was rushed to St Peter's hospital feeling 'lucky to be alive'. The electricity board later described him as 'extremely stupid'!

Treading grapes

Mrs Toni Gemmoni had never forgotten the feel of squashed fruit between her bare toes as she trod the grapes in her father's vineyard in Italy when she was a child. She came to England in 1960 and was determined that one day she would make her own wine in the traditional way. In 1972 she brought some vines back to England from Italy and festooned them around the rafters above her carport. When the fruit ripened, she put them into a traditional wooden bowl and proceeded to tread the grapes in the old-fashioned way with her bare feet.

Cliff at Christ Church

In September Cliff Richard spoke to a packed congregation at Christ Church. He explained that he became a Christian in 1965 and since then his faith had grown stronger. He had often travelled overseas to see the work done by the Christian relief organisation, TEAR Fund (The Evangelical Alliance Relief Fund). After speaking, he sang a number of popular gospel songs and signed autographs for many of his young fans.

Open for business

In October the Duchess of Kent officially opened the new shopping complex in the centre of Woking by unveiling a plaque. She was accompanied by Terry Malloy, mayor of Woking, Mrs Marnie du Boisson, the High Sheriff of Surrey, and Cranley Onslow, Woking's MP.

Curtain up

The new theatre that was built in the Centre Halls complex was to seat 230 and was to be named after Rhoda McGaw, the former chairman of Woking Council. It would be known as the Rhoda McGaw theatre.

1976

Artistic success

Local artist Alwyn Crawshaw's painting *Wet and Windy* was voted fifth in a nationwide popularity poll and at his first attempt he made it into the top ten prints of the year.

Wet and Windy shows two horses struggling against the wind. Behind the man guiding the plough, a bare tree emphasised the bleakness of the day. The artist photographed and sketched heavy farm horses working at Slocock's nursery and used them in several paintings, including *Wet and Windy*.

On the BBC television programme, *Nationwide*, Oswald Gallaway, clerk to the fine-art trade-guild, said that *Wet and Windy* was his favourite out of those submitted.

The show must go on

Mrs Kay Spurrier (63) had been one of the founder members of the Knaphill Players. She enjoyed treading the boards and had a part in *Shadow in the Sun* by

Morris McLoughlin, which was being performed at the Knaphill community centre. On the last night of the play, she collapsed on stage. The cast carried on with the production not knowing that, sadly, Mrs Spurrier had died on the way to hospital.

Olympic manager

Mr Doug Goodman from Sheerwater was appointed manager of the British Olympic team, which was to take part in the Montreal Olympics. He had already managed the British team at the Commonwealth Games.

King of the jungle

Shane, a 14-month-old lion cub, belonged to Ron Voice, a car-hire operator who lived in Maybury Road. The animal, which weighed fourteen stone, occupied an old double-decker bus. The two were inseparable and one day, when Mr Voice drove to the Chertsey Road garage, he tethered his pet to the bumper of his van. While he was in the garage, Mrs Poppy Hull, wearing a leopard-skin coat, walked down the road on her way to work.

Shane was attracted by the leopard skin. Perhaps he thought he was back in the jungle. He bounded after Mrs Hull dragging the bumper behind him. By the time he reached her, she was walking up the steps of her office. Undeterred, Shane pounced, knocked her to the ground and stood over her.

Mr Voice, realising what had happened, rushed to the scene but his pet was in a playful mood and objected to being separated from his 'playmate'. Voice assured Mrs Hull that Shane was 'only playing' and would not hurt her. He eventually managed to free her from her burden. The lady was not amused. She was uninjured but was treated for shock and later said that she would not wear her leopard-skin coat while Shane was still around.

The matter did not end there. The police were called and charges against Ron Voice were considered. Woking got some unwelcome publicity and Kenneth Kendall ended his nine o'clock news bulletin on the BBC with the words, 'Be careful what you wear in Woking.'

Cranley Onslow, Woking's MP, was at that time sponsoring a private member's bill that would require anyone keeping a dangerous pet to obtain a licence from the council. He told the *Jimmy Young Show* that he was not happy that a lion 'was stalking Woking's streets'.

Woking Borough Council was also concerned and, along with the local police, applied to the High Court for an injunction to have Shane caged and chained. This provoked a reaction from some animal lovers. Two young women who had worked for Mr Voice declared that Shane was 'warm and cuddly'. They organised a petition to protect him from 'official victimisation' and obtained 700 signatures. Mr Voice meanwhile planned to leave Woking and take his pet to a 'secret hideaway' because of the 'harassment'. 'Nothing will separate me from Shane,' he announced.

The application to control Shane was heard in chambers by the High Court judge, Justice Templeman, himself a resident of Woking. After hearing expert evidence that the lion could turn dangerous, he banned Shane's owner from exercising his pet in any public place unless it was securely caged and he was with the animal. Because the lion had apparently been moved, the judge ordered the area to be extended beyond Woking.

Curtain goes down

In March the Boys' Grammar School performed its fifty-fifth and final play, *A Man's House* by John Drinkwater. It dealt with a topical situation – a family split by differences as the younger generation rebelled against their parents. Ian Alexander, who had produced the last twenty-seven plays, was to retire at the end of the school year and pursue a new career as a minister of the United Reformed Church.

He had been interested in drama since he played his first role as a page in *As You Like It* while he was still at school. He took part in a number of school and university plays and became interested in producing plays. He even contemplated a career on the stage but felt he had made the right decision in deciding to teach as he could use his talents but avoid the 'rat race' of the commercial theatre. He started to teach English in the Grammar School in 1945.

The only other producer was Reg Church, who had directed the very first play, *Twelfth Night*, in 1918 and so started the tradition. He continued to direct until 1949 when Mr Alexander took over. Many past pupils and former staff attended the last performance. Among them was Terry Hands, assistant director of the Royal Shakespeare Company. He had first become interested in drama through starring in the Grammar School plays. The mayor and mayoress were guests of honour at the party that followed the final performance.

1977

Dickie's pal

On 27 April Lord Louis Mountbatten was the subject of *This is Your Life*. One of those interviewed on the programme was Captain Charles Drake of Knowle Hill, Woking. He had been a shipmate of Lord Louis and they had both joined the Royal Navy in 1913 when they were thirteen. They trained together and remained friends.

Captain Drake served on Churchill's staff and during that time saw a lot of 'Dickie', who was chief of combined operations. After retiring from the Navy, he became a stockbroker and moved to Woking in 1954. He was delighted to be asked to appear on the programme.

Photographic success

Colonel Mike Scott, holder of the Military Cross, retired from the army in 1967. For some years he was president of the Woking Photographic Society and in 1977 was admitted to the fellowship of the Royal Photographic Society of Great Britain. All of Colonel Scott's eighteen prints were published in the society's journal. This was very rare and was a great honour.

Pope's message

In June the Pope sent a personal message to canon Christopher Aston and the parishioners of St Dunstan's Roman Catholic church; this was to mark the twenty-fifth anniversary of the canon's ordination. He had lived in Woking for five years. The Pope gave his 'grace and abundance upon the canon on this joyful occasion'. He also extended his blessing to 'the entire parish of St Dunstan's and to all sharing in the celebration of the anniversary'.

On the Sunday, packed congregations attended two jubilee services led by Cardinal Sebastiano Gaggio who had been granted special permission from the Pope to fly over for the occasion. A mass was said for the Queen as it was also her silver jubilee. At the morning service 120 English parishioners were confirmed and in the afternoon it was the turn of seventy-five Italian children whose homes were in Woking.

Fake!

Mayford Historical Society was delighted when Anthony Bathurst informed them that he had unearthed an authentic nineteenth-century Woking diary. The society published it under the title *And so to Mainford*; over two thousand copies were circulated and some were sold.

However, Les Moore, who taught history at Horsell High School, was not happy. He did some research and discovered that the 'diary' had been concocted by Bathurst and was a fake. It was withdrawn from circulation but historian John Baker was still not impressed. He wished it to be put on record that *And so to Mainford* was a work of fiction. He was concerned that if this was not done, future historians might accept it as genuine.

Silver jubilee

Celebrations for the Queen's silver jubilee started with a service in Christ Church conducted by the vicar, Peter Searles. It was attended by the mayor and mayoress, Mr and Mrs Tony Allenby, Woking's MP and Lady June Onslow and other members of the Borough Council. Standard bearers led their organisations up the aisle and the sermon was given by Reverend Philip Gardener of Pyrford.

The weather outside was wet and cold but it did not dampen the enthusiasm of the crowds who waved their flags and cheered the grand jubilee procession of floats decorated in red, white and blue as they made their way from Lakeview to Wheatsheaf Common. This was followed by a fancy-dress parade. The youngest 'fancy dresser' was 'Miss Russell Road 1977' who wore a Union Jack and a sash bearing her title. At only twenty months, she had to be carried by her mother but she favoured the cheering crowds with a beaming smile.

In spite of the weather, celebrations were still held all over the area. Thousands flocked to Kingfield football ground to take part in the Woking family day out although most had left by five o'clock as the rain showed no sign of stopping. Sadly, many of the street parties had to adjourn to nearby village halls or church halls.

One couple whose patriotism was definitely not 'rained off' was Ginger and Sheila Duffill of South Road, Horsell. It was Sheila's idea to paint a Union Jack on their six-foot-square garage door. They spent a week happily slapping red, white and blue paint on it and, when they had completed their wok of art, they were very pleased with it.

1978

Bogus doctor

Fifty-year-old Sydney Noble had perfected his impersonation of a doctor. Using a variety of names, he was meticulous in his research. Having identified suitable gullible old ladies, he called on them, oozing authority. Once inside the house, it was a simple matter to drug his victim and then steal any valuables he could find. He committed at least fifty such crimes.

During one of his jaunts, he stayed at the Cotteridge Hotel in Woking. Then he made a mistake. He left without paying the bill and two suitcases were found in his room. Although he had registered under one of his aliases – Morris – the police were able to trace him and he was eventually charged.

Jim fixed it

Neil Thompson of St John's was addicted to *Dr Who*. He always watched the programme and, because he was fond of dogs, he was especially attracted to the robot dog K9. He wrote to Jimmy Saville to ask if Jim could possibly 'fix it' for him to meet K9. Neil was lucky. Out of the 1,000 requests that the entertainer normally received during a series of *Jim'll Fix It*, Neil's was one of those chosen.

He was too excited to eat anything before he travelled to the BBC studio in Shepherd's Bush for the show. After a short rehearsal, he was eventually introduced to K9 and made friends with 'him'. On the Saturday evening when the programme was shown, Neil was able to see himself with K9 before watching *Dr Who* and seeing the robot dog in action again.

The Queen at Wisley

In May the Queen visited the Royal Horticultural Gardens at Wisley. She was given a tour by the Lord Lieutenant of Surrey, Lord Hamilton of Dalzell, and his wife. The visit marked the hundredth anniversary of the first planting in the gardens and Her Majesty planted some trees in the new arboretum to commemorate the occasion. She also presented awards for long service to four gardeners, Ted Smith, Bert Pullinger, Leonard Porter and Dave Knight.

Charles at Pirbright

Prince Charles was also giving out medals. In June he visited Pirbright camp for the annual passing-out parade of the Welsh Guards. Wearing the Guards uniform, he presented a shield to Junior Colour Sergeant, Roland Oliffe, who had commanded the parade. Colour Sergeant Major Mark Clayton received a tankard for being the best junior recruit and eight other guardsmen were given long-service medals.

Editor celebrates

On 1 May a lunch was held at the Mayford Manor Hotel to celebrate the ninetieth birthday of Reg Gibbons who had lived in Woking since he was seven. He was a former editor of the *Woking News and Mail* and had first joined the paper in 1906 after leaving Maybury school at thirteen. The statutory school-leaving age had been fourteen but the authorities often turned a blind eye if students left slightly earlier.

Reg Gibbons was one of the first to join the newly formed National Union of Journalists and in 1912 became editor of the local paper, a post he held for thirty-seven years. He worked very hard, cycling round Woking to collect his stories and having little free time. He abhorred typewriters and preferred to use his own shorthand, which he would then transpose into longhand. For over fifty-eight years he wrote about his home town.

Woking's famous vet

The television actor, Peter Davison, also lived in Woking for much of his life. In 1970 his family moved from Knaphill to the outskirts of the town and in his free time he enjoyed pulling pints at his local pub, the Wheatsheaf, in Chobham Road. He attended Winston Churchill School and while still there, he acted as an amateur with the Byfleet Players.

In the new television series, *All Creatures Great and Small*, Davison played Tristan, the wild brother of Siegfried Farnon who owned the veterinary practice in Yorkshire. The real Tristan Farnon was a great help to Peter in creating his part as a vet – which was not all acting. He was genuinely horrified when told he had to look after some pigs that 'squeal a lot' and was definitely out of breath after chasing a herd of cows over the snow-covered moors. He enjoyed acting in the series and kept his short-back-and-sides 1930s hairstyle in preparation for the second series.

1979

Goldsworth Park

On 24 February, Laurence Wheeler married Lynn Stacey. A few days previously the mayor, Gordon Brown, had handed the couple the keys of the town's first starter home in Goldsworth Park. The starter homes were of basic design with bare walls and few fittings. They each had two bedrooms and a bathroom upstairs with a through lounge and kitchen downstairs. There was also space to build a garage.

Woking was one of the first councils to take up the idea of starter homes. Twenty-eight houses were put on the market at a 20 per cent discount and 163 applications were received. The new owners were selected by ballot and only Woking residents were eligible. Laurence and Lynn were the first to be drawn.

Angry young man

John Braine – author of *Room at the Top* and one of the 1950s 'angry young men' – published a biography of J. B. Priestley, whom he had always found 'supremely readable'. Although born in Yorkshire, Braine wrote the biography while living in Woking.

Royal finish

Captain Douglas Wilkins of Old Woking joined the RAF in 1942 and transferred to British Airways in 1947. He ended his flying career by piloting the Queen back from her tour of the Middle East. It was the first royal flight he had commanded and the plane touched down safely at Heathrow after its eight-hour journey from Muskat.

During the flight Wilkins introduced the crew of the VC10 to the Queen who was 'very charming and gracious'. She presented the pilot with a signed photograph of herself – a royal memento to cherish after a long flying career.

HADS

HADS sadly said goodbye to its popular venue, the Horsell parish hall, where so many 'magical' performances had taken place. Their performance of Alan Aykbourne's *Absurd Person Singular* took place in the Rhoda McGaw theatre although rehearsals continued to be held in Horsell.

The big red book

On 11 April Joyce Pearce, a Woking teacher, was the subject of the television programme *This is Your Life* and Eamon Andrews took her through a very full life with his 'big red book'. She had a degree in history from Oxford University and for a while taught that subject at Greenfield School in Woking. But her heart was not in it and she often fell asleep while teaching. This resulted in her pupils taking the chance to escape from their lesson as they 'did not wish to disturb Miss Pearce'!

Joyce Pearce had other things on her mind. She was very concerned about the plight of the many displaced persons in Europe after the second world war and in 1951 she and two other teachers founded the Ockenden Venture. They brought a small group of Polish and Latvian girls to England and educated them at Ockenden, a country house in White Rose Lane that Joyce had inherited from her mother.

The scheme was successful and more and more refugee children were brought to Ockenden and educated at Greenfield School. As the Venture grew, other centres were set up around the country as the refugee problem increased. Eventually the Ockenden Venture became Ockenden International, as it was felt that it was more appropriate to help people in their own environment. The publicity surrounding Pearce's work culminated in her appearance on *This is Your Life* when millions of television viewers learnt more about the vision of this Woking schoolteacher.

Chobham's cannon

In 1979 Chobham was eventually loaned a cannon by the Rotunda museum, Woolwich, to replace the one that had been presented to the village by the War Office in 1900.

The original cannon, a Russian twenty-four pounder, had been captured during the Crimean War. In 1853 Queen Victoria had reviewed the troops on Chobham Common and a stone cross had been erected to commemorate the occasion. It was nearly fifty years later that the cannon was presented to the village to commemorate the same occasion. Unfortunately in 1942 it was melted down for scrap to help the war effort and it was over thirty years before a replacement was found. This was mounted on a gun carriage that was an exact replica of the original and was made by local craftsmen. It was placed at the end of Chobham High Street and the silver plaque underneath it reads:

> The Chobham Cannon
> This cannon commemorates the reign of Queen Victoria and her visit to the Great Camp, Chobham Common in 1853. It replaces the original cannon which was taken away to be melted down to help the war effort in 1942. The cannon was replaced by the combined efforts of Chobham people and was installed on 12 May 1979. The barrel is on permanent loan from the Rotunda Museum, Woolwich, and the carriage, which is an exact copy of the original was built by local craftsmen.

1980

Jam on top

In January the 200,000 readers of the country's biggest rock weekly, *New Musical Express*, voted The Jam the best rock group. Their *Setting Sons* was considered the best album and Paul Weller from Maybury won the best songwriter and best guitarist awards.

The group had been formed at the end of the 1970s by Weller, Bruce Foxton and Rick Buckler. It had grown out of 'jamming' sessions at Sheerwater School. Performing first in the Woking working men's club, the band went on to produce many successful albums. They received a gold disc for selling 500,000 copies of *All Mod Cons*, a silver disc for the sale of 250,000 *Eton Rifles* and gold and silver discs for *Setting Sons*. In February, their hit single, *Going Underground*, went straight into the charts at number one – the first single to do that since 1973. The three lads from Sheerwater had put Woking on the pop-music map.

On 15 February, The Jam returned to their home town to play a charity concert of their greatest hits to an audience of 200 young people who had been lucky enough to get tickets. Around a hundred other fans – who had not been so lucky – waited outside to catch a glimpse of their idols.

Roy Castle

On 27 January Roy Castle was one of the guests at David Lodge's *Star Night* held at the Rhoda McGaw theatre. The event was to raise money for the Ockenden Venture and local performers as well as professionals took part.

Redcap award

Graham Field was in the Sheerwater army cadet force while he was at Sheerwater School; he then went on to train with the Royal Military Police at Bovington Camp in Dorset. At the passing-out parade he was presented with the provost marshal's sword for being the best junior leader in the Military Police. The presentation was made by Major General Martin Sinnatt. Graham also achieved the highest educational standard of the junior leaders and for this he won the Saunders Cup.

Family link

After fifty-one years, Fred Jordan retired from working at Unwin's printing works. His father, Thomas Jordan, had worked there before him as an engineer. Thomas Jordan had started working for the firm in 1907 and, when he retired in 1937, he had been presented with a barometer and a ceremonial chair with a plaque. Fred inherited these in 1976 when his father died. Sadly, the family connection would not continue as Fred's son chose to work in electronics at Farnborough.

Destined for Auschwitz

In July, Ulrich Otto Friedrich Sieger died of cancer. He had been head of English at Winston Churchill School. Born in Germany, he grew up in Eissen near the river Rhine. Then, when he was thirteen, his father was arrested and dragged off to Auschwitz. Ulrich was destined for the same horror but with the help of Captain Stevens, a naval attaché at the British embassy, he was smuggled out of the country. He went to live with the captain's family in Wales and learnt English at the Welsh Bible School near Swansea.

He trained as a teacher and moved to Woking where he taught at Goldsworth Secondary before becoming head of English at Winston Churchill.

Attempted murder

John Gale, from Horsell, was not happy in his marriage. He complained to his friend, David Bale, that his Italian wife, Maria, refused to cook his meals and denied him his conjugal rights. Bale was sympathetic and was under the impression that Gale wanted him to do something about it.

Gale took a mistress, Judy Greenwood, and one night while they were in bed together in the marital home, David Bale let himself into the house, went up to Maria's bedroom and attacked her while she slept. She woke up and was able to fight him off; he fled, but not before she had recognised him.

Bale was arrested and charged with attempted murder. At his trial at the Old Bailey, he told the court that John Gale had paid him £50 to murder his wife. He was jailed for nine years.

John Gale was acquitted of attempting to murder his wife and Bale's sentence was later reduced to four years. He had lied at his trial. He had *not* been paid to murder Maria and he had certainly had no intention of killing her. He had only wanted to frighten her.

1981

Closure of Brookwood

In 1981 – to the relief of many Woking residents – Brookwood, the town's psychiatric hospital, closed. It had been opened in June 1867 as the Surrey County Pauper Lunatic Asylum. Conditions in the early days were stark and followed the pattern in the rest of the country. However, over the years the treatment of the mentally ill became more humane.

One interesting development was the formation in June 1874 of a hospital dancing-club. Dancing was used not only as recreation but, interestingly, as part of patient treatment. The club, probably the oldest in the country, flourished until the closure of the hospital.

Job for a ferret

David Overy (12) of Mayford had a pet ferret and was delighted to be asked to appear on the children's television show *Ace Report*. A car collected him and his pet and took them to the studio. He learned that ferrets were very useful in the laying of cables. If there was a bend in the tunnel, the cable was attached to the tail of the ferret which was then encouraged to chase a piece of ham. According to Thames Television, this was normal practice; the post office also used ferrets when installing underground cables.

Royal wedding

Wednesday, 29 July was the wedding day of Prince Charles and Lady Diana Spencer. The streets of Woking were decorated with patriotic bunting and shops vied with each other to produce attractive window displays. Sheerwater's youth organisations created a huge royal greeting card with a picture of the happy couple on the front. Representatives were chosen to take it to Buckingham Palace and deliver it personally.

The day itself was quiet as most Woking residents were watching the historic event on television. Later there were street parties and fancy-dress parades as Woking celebrated the wedding and toasted Charles and his bride in the pubs.

Epworth choir on television

On Sunday, 2 August, the Epworth choir starred on the BBC Television programme, *Home on Sunday*. Some of the hymns were chosen by the speaker of the House of Commons, the Right Honourable George Thomas.

100 up

On Saturday, 19 September Roy Castle stepped out of a helicopter on Wheatsheaf Common. He had come to launch an appeal on behalf of the Church Army, which was celebrating its hundredth anniversary. £1,000 had been raised by local residents towards the appeal and pupils from the Queen Elizabeth II School handed Roy a cheque on behalf of their school.

He signed autographs in Robinson's department store in Chertsey Road and the queue stretched from the top of the second storey, down the stairs to the street. In the town square he presented some books to the head librarian, Miss Rachel Buxton. They had been donated by the Church Army to the town library.

The town square was crowded and Castle entertained the crowd by playing 'When the Saints Go Marching In' on a trombone once owned by Wilson Carlile, the founder of the Church Army movement. The Marie Carlile Church Army Home in Coley Avenue was named after the founder's sister. The police entered into the spirit of the day by 'arresting' the entertainer for 'disturbing the peace'.

1982

Band disbands

The Jam disbanded in 1982. Paul Weller moved away from the area but still retained links with his home town and often visited his mother in Woking.

Secret wedding

On 7 January Heather Hales from Woking married the famous conductor, André Previn. It was a secret ceremony at a register office in Pittsburgh, Pennsylvania. Heather was a talented glass engraver and in 1976 the Guild of Glass Engravers held an open exhibition in Middlesex where two decanters she had engraved were exhibited.

She first met Previn in 1977 when she was living in Horsell Rise with her husband, actor Michael Jayston. She became friendly with the conductor's third wife, Mia Farrow, and engraved a wine glass as a gift for her. André Previn and Mia Farrow were divorced in 1979. When he and Heather met again, they fell in love. Both were divorced and decided to keep their wedding plans secret.

Bookworm

Joanne Farmer was eleven and went to Greenfield School. She was obsessed with Lord Nelson and for the past four years had spent as much time as possible reading about him. On 16 January the BBC sent a car to take her and her parents to the Shepherd's Bush studio. She was taking part in the final of *Swap Shop Mastermind*, hosted by Noel Edmonds. It was a tense final but, with her wide knowledge of Lord Nelson, Joanne won and was given an encyclopaedia as her prize.

Phantom cockerel

Residents of Manor Road in Horsell objected to having their beauty sleep disturbed by the raucous crowing of a cockerel who could not tell the time. It seemed to have no idea that it was only supposed to crow at dawn. Its favourite time for opening its mouth was between two and three o'clock in the morning when all good citizens were sleeping. Then it decided to herald afternoon teatime by emitting its unnatural sounds.

No one had ever seen it although many people had certainly heard it. The help of Dick Ford, manager of Woking car parks, was enlisted. He owned a poultry park and knew the ways of his feathered flock. He denied that the errant cockerel belonged to him although he too had heard it at odd times throughout the day. He diligently combed the village looking for it but the phantom cockerel was too clever. It was never found.

Panic stations

On Monday, 1 February a passenger, boarding the ten-thirty train from Woking station to Waterloo, noticed a small metal box on an empty seat. There were wires protruding from it. Because of the heightened security as a result of recent IRA bombs, the passenger left the train and reported the box to a porter who wasted no time in alerting the police; they arrived promptly and evacuated the station within minutes. Spencer Neville, Woking's chief superintendent of police, rushed to the scene.

All the railway lines through Woking were closed, paralysing train services to London and the South of England. A barrier was erected around the station, and the subway linking the north of Woking to the south was closed. Frustrated pedestrians had to walk half a mile to get from one side of the station to the other. Traffic chaos soon followed.

The police were concerned about some German lettering on the 'bomb' and called an army bomb-disposal-unit, which arrived with a remote-control 'wheelbarrow' robot-bomb-prober. This was wheeled forward to scan the 'bomb' for any explosive content. The experts watched carefully the closed-circuit television pictures it sent back.

They studied the screen for half an hour. They could see a battery pack with metal casing and wires protruding from it. They eventually identified the object as a discarded battery pack used for camera flashes. The 'bomb' contained no explosives. It was harmless. Woking could return to normal after proving itself up to dealing with an emergency.

Diamond jubilee

On 6 February a dinner was held to celebrate the sixtieth birthday of Horsell Amateur Dramatic Society in Horsell parish hall, where many productions had been staged. Among the ninety guests were Phyllis Drower who had starred in HADS very first production, *The Man from Toronto,* and Irene Hutchence, who had been a member for fifty-five years.

Television personality Patrick Moore, who had also been a member, was not able to attend the dinner but was at the first night of the jubilee production, *Times Twenty*, a musical set in the 1920s, the decade in which the group was founded. It was written by Woking resident, Colin Campbell. The play was performed at the Rhoda McGaw theatre in March.

Superstar

Brian Hooper from Sheerwater was the former British and Commonwealth pole-vaulting champion. On 12 February he won the prestigious *Superstars* title on BBC Television.

As one door closes . . .

The Queen Elizabeth 11 School closed its doors for the last time at the end of the school year. There had been much opposition to this and Cranley Onslow had even pleaded with the education secretary, Sir Keith Joseph, to keep it open. But he was overruled. At the same time Sheerwater School also closed. In September, a new school, Bishop David Brown, opened on the Sheerwater site. Pupils from both schools attended the new school, which had 720 pupils.

1983

Pooch ate bingo ticket

Woking Borough's mace bearer, Rob Simms, and his wife, Millie, were the most disappointed couple in Woking. Duke, their Alsatian dog, had eaten their bingo ticket. Because they had no ticket to show, they missed out on a share of a £40,000 bingo jackpot in *The Sun*.

Opening of civic offices

On 20 April, Richard, Duke of Gloucester, unveiled a plaque to open the new civic offices. It rained all day but crowds still gathered for the occasion. The Duke was greeted by the Lord Lieutenant of Surrey, Lord Hamilton of Dalzell, the mayor of Woking, Mrs Elizabeth Butler, and the chief executive, Rodney Dew. As an architect, the Duke was interested in the construction of the building. The borough architects, Jim Boyle and Ray Freeland, took him on a tour of the building. The pedestrian precinct was named Gloucester Square in honour of the occasion and the building was dedicated by Peter Searle, vicar of Christ Church.

Lie led to murder

Susan Chappell was a talented musician and a member of the National Youth Orchestra. Until her marriage she lived with her parents in Woking. She met

John Lennox – a baker from Durham – one summer when they were both working in Bognor Regis at Butlin's holiday camp.

After her marriage, she moved with her husband to Durham where she was not happy. She was classed as a snob by her new neighbours because of her 'posh' accent. The couple had a baby but the marriage was foundering and Susan took a lover, John Willis, who was more than ten years older than she was. When their secret relationship ended, she accused Willis of rape. That rankled.

When her daughter was only eighteen months old, Susan disappeared, wearing a green windcheater and pink slippers. Police all over the country searched for her. It was thought she might be trying to return to Woking and media help was enlisted. Her husband hoped that someone might have seen her and she could be persuaded to return to him.

It was not to be. Two weeks after she disappeared, Susan's body was found buried under foliage in a wooded ravine near her home. She had been murdered by her former lover, John Willis. He had shot her twice and then turned the gun on himself, leaving a suicide message scrawled on a nearby wall: 'Our love could not have lasted but I shot the lying bastard. Rape – not guilty. Murder – guilty. Sorry, Mum and family.'

Music success

Surrey County Wind Orchestra was directed by David Hamilton, the head of Woking music centre. Four girls from Woking College played in it: they were Lindsay Marns on the trumpet, Elizabeth Caton on the clarinet, Valerie Maberly on the oboe and Sarah Morley on the bassoon.

On 20 November, the orchestra, with eleven other bands, went to Westminster school to take part in a national contest sponsored by music publishers, Boosey and Hawkes. The orchestra performed Stephen Dodgson's *Symphony for Wind Orchestra* and were awarded ninety-five marks. They won first prize and received £100.

Drama in the park

There was high drama in Goldsworth Park one weekend in November. On the Friday morning Richard Colton rang the police and told them he'd barricaded himself into his house and intended to shoot himself as he had just lost his job. At the time he was under the care of the probation service and his probation officer, Mark Verity, went round to reason with him. He was unable to persuade him to relinquish his shotgun and the police decided to evacuate the area.

The siege continued for thirty hours while the police patiently negotiated with him. Eventually, on Saturday evening, Inspector Chris Saunders persuaded him to put the gun on the window ledge where it could be seen and give himself up. Colton was later admitted to hospital as an 'informal patient'.

Queen's coroner

Lieutenant Colonel George McEwan, who lived in Mayford, had been West Surrey's coroner since 1963. On 1 December he was appointed coroner to the Queen's household. He was the fifth holder of the post, which dates from 1887.

1984

A new knight

Peter Lane was made a knight in the New Year's honours list for his political services. A member of the Conservative Party's policy-making committee, he had chaired the 1983 Conservative conference. Born in Horsell, he lived in Orchard Drive and was educated at Sherborne school in Dorset. He became a chartered accountant and a local magistrate.

We are not alone

In January three independent witnesses were convinced they had seen unidentified flying objects. The first was a Chobham rugby player who was driving along Woodham Lane early one evening. Suddenly, a huge red light flashed across the sky above him and then fell and disappeared. As there was no crash, he was sure it was not an aircraft. The second witness saw the same red light but in more detail. It was in the shape of a triangle and glowed red in the sky before rapidly descending and disappearing. Once again there was no sound.

The third sighting was by an 18-year-old student and it was slightly different. She saw three bright lights hovering in the sky above the woods. They moved to the left and gradually disappeared. A few minutes later three more lights glittered above the trees before forming themselves into a huge triangle.

Were these 'visions' supernatural or was there a more rational explanation?

A new who

Science fiction was still popular on television. Peter Davison from Woking, who had played Tristan Farnon in *All Creatures Great and Small*, was cast as the new Dr Who. To celebrate the filming of the last episode of the series, he bought a £17,000 Range Rover from Trident Garages in Ottershaw.

Fiftieth anniversary

1984 was the fiftieth anniversary of Robinson's department store. Since William Robinson opened the store in 1934 it had expanded. By 1960 the company owned adjoining premises in Chertsey Road and eventually a new five-storey building was built on the original site. This incorporated offices on the top floor and a restaurant. The store was still owned by David Robinson and his sister, the second generation of Robinsons.

Reunited

In 1959 Shirley McFarlane-Rodger watched with tears in her eyes as her 2-year-old, Ricky, sailed away to Australia. She would not see him again for twenty-five years. She had married Neil after a whirlwind courtship and they set up home in Manchester. Ricky was born but when he was only four months old, Neil decided to emigrate to Australia. Shirley was not happy there and returned to England with Ricky.

Unfortunately she found it impossible to cope as a single mother and when Neil's sister suggested she would take Ricky back to Australia with her, Shirley agreed. But Neil was not interested in the toddler and put him in a children's home. Shirley never got over her loss. She wrote repeatedly to Ricky but received no reply. She moved to Pyrford where she became agoraphobic and had to stop working.

But Rick had never forgotten his mother and eventually he traced her. Her correspondence was resumed and at last Ricky was able to visit England to meet the mother he had not seen for a quarter of a century.

Horse show

The Crown Life Assurance Company, one of Woking's largest employers, sponsored several showjumping events at the Royal International Horse Show in Birmingham. The Crown Life Assurance Championship was won by Malcolm Pyrah on Towerlands Anglezarke; the award was presented by Princess Anne, president of the British Olympic Association.

She was escorted by Mr Allan Duggin, managing director of the Woking Crown Life Assurance Company. He and his wife – together with other executives of the Woking company – were later present at a dinner that was also attended by Princess Anne and her husband, Captain Mark Philips.

1985

Bizarre anniversary

This year marked the hundredth anniversary of the first cremation to take place in Woking. It deserves to be noted as Woking has the bizarre reputation of having grown as a town partly because it built the first crematorium in England. This was because it had a railway line available to ferry the dead from the capital to their final resting place. Another reason was that land that had originally been bought to use for the Brookwood cemetery was not used for that purpose and was eventually sold to developers.

Because it was becoming more difficult to find space to bury the dead in London, it was necessary to acquire land outside the capital. In 1878 land near St John's village had been bought for £200 by Sir Henry Thompson, surgeon to Queen Victoria, and the founder of the Cremation Society. Although cremation was still illegal in England, a crematorium – including the sixty-foot-high chimney – was completed on the site in 1879.

To test its function, Sir Henry ordered the body of a horse to be cremated and he closely watched the proceedings. He was satisfied with the result but the local residents protested and Parliament still refused to allow human cremation. Then five years later Mr Justin Stephen made an historic speech in support of a Mr Price who had had his child cremated in defiance of the law.

The following year, in 1885, the first official cremation took place in Woking and by the end of the century nearly 2,000 cremations had taken place. Among those cremated in Woking were: Dr Barnardo, founder of the famous children's home; Thomas Hardy, the novelist; Prince Arthur, Duke of Connaught, son of Queen Victoria.

Queen visits

On 8 July the Queen visited Gordon's Boys' School, of which she was patron, to give the prizes at the school's centenary speech-day and to present the colours at the parade service. The school, in West End near Chobham, was founded in 1885 by Queen Victoria as a memorial to General Gordon who had been murdered in Khartoum earlier that year. A copy of the famous painting, *Gordon's Last Stand*, hangs at the back of the chapel.

To commemorate the anniversary, the school commissioned a new painting. The artist was Terence Cuneo. The painting showed Gordon presenting his journal to the master of the steamship *Bordein*. Unfortunately the artist had not been given enough information and he clad Gordon in the uniform of a *British*, instead of a *Turkish*, general. The presence of three British soldiers in their scarlet uniforms was also incorrect as there were no British soldiers anywhere near the area at the time. The artist repainted Gordon's uniform blue, blocked out two of the soldiers and transformed the third one into a scarlet-liveried palace servant.

Also published in the centenary year was a history of the Gordon's Boys' School by Lieutenant Colonel Derek Boyd, entitled *The Gordon Heritage*.

New HQ

The Sheerwater Scout group had its roots in 1956 when eight boys set up a cub group and appointed a leader. They became Scouts and the group went on to become one of Woking's most successful Scout groups. On 30 March their new headquarters was opened by the mayor of Woking, John Jewson. The ceremony was presided over by London's town crier and 400 Scouts and leaders then enjoyed a celebration supper in their new hall.

War in Pyrford?

In September Pyrford residents were startled by six loud explosions which were also heard several miles away. Elderly people were terrified when their houses shook. Had world war three started? No. A film crew from Pinewood Studios had set up camp on nearby farmland to film *Gunbus*, a first world war adventure, using authentic fighter planes as well as fantasy machines.

The explosions, which jammed police switchboards, were produced from powder mixed with a small amount of gelignite. The crew did not expect the noise to travel so far and apologised profusely for the disturbance that had been caused.

Wang in Woking

Also in September, a delegation from Beijing in the People's Republic of China paid a visit to Woking. It was the first such visit and was a fact-finding mission about transportation. Led by Mr Wang Dekong, director of the Institute of Comprehensive Transportation, the Chinese were welcomed by the mayor, Pat Bohling, and taken on a tour of the civic offices.

1986

Night light

Mr Neil Whitehorn of Goldsworth Park complained to the council that a new street light outside his window was so bright it enabled him to read in bed without switching on his light. He demanded a 50 per cent reduction in his rates. The Valuation Court awarded him a reduction of £10 but said it would be withdrawn should the council remove the offending light.

Sheerwater was also having 'light' problems. Because of the recent 'freeze', the old water tanks had burst and houses were flooded with water cascading out of the light sockets and down the walls.

Drop-in centre

A drop-in centre for the elderly was opened in High Street. It was named after Marjorie Richardson, the former chairman of Woking Urban District Council. A tireless volunteer, she had started the annual Christmas dinner for lonely folk in Woking. In April, a lunch was given to celebrate her retirement, after thirty years, from voluntary work. Although she intended to move to Dorset, she promised to return to visit the drop-in centre that bears her name. The centre is open every day except Sunday and 'caters for all retired and disabled people'. It serves drinks and snacks and also arranges parties for special occasions.

Di at Byfleet

On 11 March the Princess of Wales arrived in Byfleet to open St Mary's day centre. She was met by the Lord Lieutenant of Surrey, Lord Hamilton, and Mrs Pat Bohling, mayor of Woking. Local residents turned out to see her and she did a 'walkabout' for several minutes. Mrs Bohling said that for her it was 'a dream come true'. The Princess had 'a great affinity with the elderly and was very complimentary about the centre'.

On track

On 5 April a crowd of 2,000 gathered to watch Pat Bohling cut the ribbon to open Woking Athletic Club's new all-weather track in Sheerwater. Founders of the club, which was celebrating its silver jubilee, and many sporting personalities were present including Maria Hartman, president of the Women's Athletic Association and top international athlete, Bill Nankeville, who had lived in Woking and did some of his training in the town.

Maggie's surprise

Mrs Thatcher, the Prime Minister, paid a surprise visit to Woking in April. In recognition of his work for the party, she presented a signed scroll to Christopher Meyer, the retiring chairman of Woking constituency

Conservative Association. She also praised Mr Cranley Onslow, Woking's MP, for his work as chairman of the backbench 1922 committee.

Security was tight because of our close ties with America, which had recently bombed Libya, and retaliation was feared. Mrs Thatcher told her listeners, 'Europe would not be free today but for the British and Americans standing together.' The new constituency chairman, Donald Porter, presented her with a cheque for £2,000 for party funds.

1987

The Woking Cosa Nostra

During the second world war there was an Italian prisoner-of-war camp in West Byfleet and, after the war, many Italians married local girls and made their homes in the area. Among those who set up home in Woking were members of the Sicilian Mafia. The town was ideal for their nefarious activities. It was near the airports, motorways made it easy to reach the coast and London was only twenty-five miles away.

Mafia godfather Pasquale Caruana set up the Woking connection from his luxury home in Hook Heath and adapted the house to suit his 'business'. Caruana and Francesco Siracusa of Westfield Road ran a store in Mitcham, which imported furniture. However, the imports were not what they seemed. Much of the furniture contained hidden supplies of drugs and a warehouse on Brooklands industrial estate near Woking was also used for storing the illegal merchandise. Suitcases full of cash from their drug trafficking and money laundering were deposited in Barclays Bank in Knaphill. The bank, however, respected its clients' confidentiality and denied any connection with the Mafia.

Eventually, the police got close to Caruana and, with his English wife, Shelagh, and two young sons, he fled to Canada leaving Shelagh's father to sell the house. Although Caruana had left Woking, the Mafia connection was still alive in the town. Godfather Francesco Di Carlo lived in another luxury mansion in Horsell Rise. This was surrounded by high hedges and the gates had been boarded up. The neighbours considered this 'very unfriendly'.

Di Carlo was not as fortunate as Caruana and he was eventually arrested for heroin trafficking. In March 1987 he was tried at the Old Bailey; in spite of attempting to silence witnesses, he was found guilty and sentenced to twenty-five years. He was also fined £250,000 and ordered to pay £50,000 costs; the court did not find it easy to obtain the money as a recent Drug Trafficking Act prevented the sale of a defendant's house to pay his fine or costs.

Although he and his wife Guiseppina had separated in 1985, she and her two daughters had been living in the Horsell Rise mansion. After her husband was jailed, Guiseppina and her daughters left for Sicily, driving secretly at night so as not to attract attention.

Di Carlo would not be free for twenty-five years but there was someone in Woking ready to step into his shoes. This was Salvatori Di Prima, who had decorated Di Carlo's home in Horsell Rise. Di Carlo became fond of the younger man and adopted him as his son. When Di Carlo was jailed, he handed over the Woking connection to Di Prima, who was instructed to keep a low profile as a manager of a wine bar in Mitcham, although still living in Russell Road in Woking.

But Di Prima was greedy and decided he could work alone. He knew that £50,000 was buried in a safe in the garden of the Horsell Rise house and he stole the money. With its effective intelligence service, the Mafia soon discovered this and passed a sentence of death upon the 31-year-old drug baron.

However, before the execution could be carried out, Di Prima was caught by British Customs. He had neglected to keep a low profile and it had not been difficult to follow him. He had recruited Robert Patrick and Sharon Walters to smuggle cannabis into England from Spain. They were to pose as holidaymakers and, to give them authenticity, a tiny baby was borrowed so they would appear a normal family.

But Customs were already on his trail. After he had met the couple in Plymouth and retrieved the package they had brought from Spain, he was arrested. In March 1987 he was found guilty at Exeter Crown Court of masterminding the plot to smuggle drugs into England and was sentenced to seven years in jail.

1988

Ritz demolished

The old Ritz cinema, which had been a bingo hall for fifteen years, was finally demolished to make way for new office buildings.

Hijacked!

Mr Peter Bartlam from Mt Hermon Road in Woking and his girlfriend, Jacqui Foss, expected to have an uneventful flight home after their trip to Thailand. But it was not to be. About an hour before they were due to land, Bartlam was woken from sleep by a man beside him shouting, 'Get your head down. We're going to kill everyone.'

It was the start of a week of terror. The hijackers were educated and intelligent. They knew exactly what they were doing and were obviously well trained. There was no physical violence but the passengers and crew were subjected to a continual psychological battle. The men ran up and down the aisle waving guns in each hand. One sat with a grenade in his mouth. They raided suitcases for clothes to wear to confuse any rescuers and made passengers frequently change seats.

Jacqui Foss was eventually set free but her boyfriend was tied up and a grenade was held to his head. After three days, he and another man were taken to the front of the plane and told to put their hands behind their heads; Bartlam was convinced he was going to be shot.

But, to his amazement, he was released and as he left the plane one of the hijackers said politely, 'Sorry to have inconvenienced you.' Peter Bartlam had been in the hijacked plane for fifty-three hours but other passengers were still held hostage. He was relieved to see Woking again.

The Basingstoke canal

1988 was the bicentenary of the start of the construction of the Basingstoke canal. It had been started in 1788 in Woodham where it joined the Wey navigation. Although the town of Woking did not exist at that time, the area that is now Woking and its surrounding villages played a part in the development of the canal. Many of the bricks that line the locks were made in the Woking area although some of the original ones have been replaced. Apparently in the eighteenth century a Mr Wildgoose of Horsell was instrumental in pointing the builders in the direction of the best local brick-clay.

Railway town

This year was also the hundred-and-fiftieth anniversary of the opening of the first railway station in Woking. It was on 19 May 1838 that the first train with its four hundred VIP passengers left Vauxhall to travel to Woking, which became the terminus of the first railway line in Surrey. In 1838 the station consisted only of a wooden platform and two sheds. As there was no suitable inn in the area to provide sustenance for the passengers, some tents were erected in which 'an elegant collation' was provided.

Woking Palace

Concerned that Woking was about to lose one of its most famous historical sites, the borough council bought the land on which Woking Palace had stood. Originally the manor house, it had been transformed into a royal palace by

Lady Margaret Beaufort, the mother of Henry VII. Set in a part of the royal forest of Windsor, it was visited frequently by Henry VIII and at least two of his wives.

After Henry died, the palace fell into disrepair as his successors visited it rarely. Then James I presented it to Sir Edward Zouch in 1620. Sir Edward was not impressed with it and demolished it; he used some of the bricks to build himself a new residence at Hoe Bridge Place. The palace area continued to decay until the council bought it. It will now be protected and archaeologists and historians will have the opportunity to discover more about the site. Although the area is not open to the public, open days are held occasionally and Iain Wakeford, the local historian, takes guided tours around it.

1989

Woking's twin

After the second world war, there was a movement to promote friendship and understanding between nations. In 1957 the Treaty of Rome highlighted this and the twinning initiative started to flourish. When England joined the European Community in 1972, she too became interested in twinning and in the early 1980s the Woking Town Twinning Association was formed.

Overtures to Amstelveen in Holland were made in 1983 but it was not until 1989 that Woking signed her first charter of friendship with the Dutch city, which is situated seven miles south of Amsterdam. Established in 1278 as a fishing and farming community, its peat-digging industry gave rise to its name, which means 'a watery place with peat'. It began to expand in the seventeenth century and today it is a lively prosperous community and, like Woking, has a diverse ethnic population. Since twinning with Amstelveen, many Woking organisations have formed links with similar groups in the Dutch city and a number of exchange visits have been arranged.

Earthquake

Peter Richmond, an electronics engineer, had attended Woking Boys' Grammar School. When he married Kate, a fashion model, who had been a pupil at the Girls' Grammar School, they moved to California to live. In October 1989 Peter's parents, Tony and Vera, who lived in Kettlewell Drive, Woking, visited them for the first time. While there, they experienced the earthquake that rocked San Francisco.

They were sitting on the veranda enjoying their afternoon cup of tea when suddenly there was a sound like the approach of an express train. They all rushed out on to the lawn away from the buildings. It was difficult to stand as the ground was rumbling and heaving like a storm at sea. The quake lasted for about thirty seconds and then for a short while everything was calm. The family was thinking of returning to the house when the earth trembled again.

Eventually the tremors ceased. The house did not appear to be damaged but inside it looked as though a burglar had ransacked it. Crockery and ornaments had been thrown around and smashed, furniture was upturned and the cooker and fridge had 'walked'.

Peter Richmond was at work and it was not until the following day that he was able to get home. His wife and parents were relieved to see him as the communication system had broken down and they had not been able to make contact. Over the next three days there were more tremors but they were not serious. However, it must have been a relief for Tony and Vera Richmond to arrive back in Woking where the ground was stable.

Death of Sir Peter Lamdin

Sir Peter Lamdin, director of Woking Funeral Services, died in October. His father had established the business in 1929 and he had joined it in 1945.

Success on the cards

In their centenary year, Woking Cardinals reached the second round of the FA Cup by defeating Slough 2–1 in a spectacular match. They were watched by a thousand spectators of all ages, who were delighted by their team's prowess. Woking had not been defeated all season. They had won sixteen games and drawn three.

Death of Mrs Bedser

On 18 December, Florence Bedser died at Beechcroft hospital. The mother of the famous cricketing Bedser twins, she was ninety-seven. She was the widow of Arthur Bedser who, as a builder, had constructed many of Woking's public buildings. The funeral was held on 22 December at All Saints Church, Woodham.

1990

Nine-hundredth anniversary

1990 was celebrated as the nine-hundredth anniversary of St Peter's Church in Old Woking, the original Woking parish church. It is still the mother church of the borough of Woking. The exact date of its founding is not known but the earliest records show that in AD 625 a minster was founded in the area by Brordar, a nobleman. Then, 120 years later, King Offa made a grant to the church. The Domesday Book recorded that Woking had a church and during the reign of William the Conqueror a new church was built on the site of the wooden Saxon one.

Over the centuries the building continually changed. During the reign of James I a gallery was added by Sir Edward Zouch and a huge, three-decker pulpit was installed so that worshippers in the gallery could see the preacher. On 27 August 1627 Charles I visited the church; he heard Henry Lesly, 'one of His Majesties Chaplaines in Ordinarie' preach on being born again. The sermon lasted three hours and covered thirty-one pages.

To celebrate the anniversary, various events were planned throughout the year; there was an exhibition in the church illustrating its history and giving details of its activities. Among the exhibits was the original script of the sermon preached to Charles I. In April the artist Tim Pollard signed copies of his sketch of the church and in July there was a flower festival. The annual civic service, usually held in Christ Church, was held in St Peter's and there were concerts throughout the year culminating in a carol concert in December.

Unusual pets

Nigel and Jackie Holman owned a flock of sheep and were planning to buy more. However, when they visited a Welsh farm, they met a llama. It kissed Nigel and he fell in love with it so, instead of buying sheep, they bought two llamas and named them Clementine and Lorenzo. They made ideal pets as they didn't bark or bite and they did not even 'chatter' to each other but communicated by watching the other's ears twitch.

The Holmans enjoyed taking their pets for a walk along Horsell Rise. Llamas were becoming popular as pets among the jet set. Apparently Michael Jackson owned one. When not walking, they grazed on the back lawn and would be sheared once a year; the 'wool' could be hand-knitted into luxurious sweaters.

Girls at Gordons

In September, for the first time, girls were admitted to Gordon's Boys' School and the name was changed to Gordon's School.

Police station opened

On 18 October, the Duke of Gloucester opened the new police station and court complex on the site of the Boys' Grammar School. The original building with

Bill's bangers

Bill Noel moved to Sheerwater in 1979 and opened a butcher's shop. He had been a butcher for forty-three years and specialised in sausages. For forty years customers had enjoyed his special sausages, made from his own recipe. This year his sausages won the speciality sausage section in a competition sponsored by the London Retail Meat Traders Association.

1991

A turn-up for the Cards

In January Tim Buzaglo scored three goals for Woking Cardinals against West Bromwich Albion inside fifteen minutes; Woking went on to win the third round FA Cup tie 4–2. It was played at West Brom's ground, the Hawthorns, and after the match, the home supporters hoisted Buzaglo aloft and paraded him round the ground in a rare show of sportsmanship. His fifteen minutes of fame attracted national interest and, for a brief spell, Woking basked in his reflected glory. He even made the headlines as far away as Thailand, in the *Bangkok Post*.

The club was the first in the Vauxhall Opel league to score four goals in a third-round match. In the fourth round Woking lost to Everton at Goodison Park on Sunday, 27 January in front of nearly 35,000 spectators. Ten thousand Woking supporters were there to cheer on their team, who played magnificently, and were given a standing ovation. The Everton manager said of them: 'They are a fine team and caused us some problems.'

Gulf War

In January Britain went to war to free Kuwait from the clutches of Saddam Hussein. Eighteen-year-old Wayne Adams, a former Horsell High School boy, was in the Coldstream Guards. At school he had been an army cadet and when he left, he joined the army and trained at Pirbright camp. He completed his training in June 1990 and had been involved in ceremonial duties in London. When the war started, he flew out to the Middle East with his regiment to set up a prisoner-of-war camp.

Gordon Girls in London

In February, in London, Gordon girls for the first time joined their male counterparts to march across Whitehall towards the statue of General Gordon in Embankment Gardens. The skirl of the pipes of the kilted Highland band attracted spectators, who watched the parade and saw the school chaplain conduct a short wreath-laying service around the statue.

1992

Drug ring smashed

In January four men were jailed after appearing at Guildford Crown Court charged with smuggling heroin into Woking and other Surrey towns. The undercover operation that finally broke the ring was masterminded from Woking police station. The information received was coordinated in the incident room by Detective Sergeant Charlie Frost.

With painstaking care, the undercover officers discovered the heroin route and set about destroying it by arresting the ringleaders. The heroin originated in Pakistan, was taken by couriers to Amsterdam and from there to London; it was finally distributed in towns in the south of England including Woking. After the success of the operation, drug-enforcement officers from agencies in Sweden and the United States visited to learn from the experiences of Woking police.

Old Woking

Old Woking celebrated its nine-hundredth anniversary by commissioning a new sign to be put up at the entrance to the village. It was made by Clive Dunning, a local craftsman, and depicted the eleventh century St Peter's Church. The Old Woking Village Association had been planning it for three years and the sign was unveiled by the vicar of St Peter's, Barry Grimster.

Peacocks opened

Friday, 10 April was an important day for Woking. The £120 million Peacocks complex was officially opened. It had been created as a result of cooperation between Woking Borough Council and the London and Edinburgh Trust. Ultimately it would consist of seven floors with a shopping complex, car park, restaurants, a crèche, cinemas and theatres. Underneath the glass dome a huge peacock, showing off its tail, stared benignly down at the visitors. The car park with spaces for 2,500 cars had direct undercover access to both the shopping and entertainment areas.

The opening was announced in the town centre by Peter Moore, London's town crier. On Friday and Saturday there was a festival atmosphere in the town. Jugglers, clowns and even a Dixieland band entertained the crowds and the Peacocks centre was declared officially open by magician Paul Daniels and his assistant, Debbie McGee. Other celebrities also visited. Among them were Helena Bonham-Carter, Gary Wilmot, Richard O'Brien and Simon Callow. Michael Aspel cut the ribbon to open Allders department store, said to be the largest in Surrey.

The first film to be shown in one of the three cinemas was Steven Spielberg's *Hook* and, to publicise it, there was a competition for the best-dressed pirate. Facilities for the hard of hearing were available in all the cinemas. Also introduced was a shopmobility scheme for disabled shoppers and those with mobility problems. The glass-fronted lifts made movement from one floor to another easy for the custom-built wheelchairs.

Over the next week over 95,000 visitors came to the new centre. Then, on 26 April, the Rhoda McGaw theatre reopened with a gala concert. To the delight of the drama groups who used it, the little theatre had remained standing amidst the rubble of demolition all around it. The concert, *Hoorah for Hollywood*, was compered by BBC Television's Rob Curling. The star performers were the Octavian Singers, a chamber choir.

In June the New Victoria theatre was officially opened by the actor, Nigel Hawthorne. It seated 1,300 and the first performance to an invited audience was of the Northern Ballet Theatre's production of *Swan Lake*, which received a standing ovation.

1993

Bride butchered

On 20 November 31-year-old Adam Tadd, in a fit of jealous frenzy, stabbed his wife of ten months sixteen times with a six-inch flick knife. The attack was so ferocious that marks from the hilt of the knife were later found on 21-year-old Jeanette's body.

Outside the locked bedroom door in Abbey Road, Horsell – where the couple lived with Jeanette's parents – the victim's mother stood helplessly while her daughter was being butchered. When the door was finally opened, Adam Tadd darted out brandishing the bloodstained knife at his distraught mother-in-law, who rushed past him to find her daughter dying.

Tadd and Jeanette Wareham had been married in January after a whirlwind romance. They had moved into her parents' house until they could buy a flat of their own. Sadly, the marriage soon ran into trouble. Adam Tadd was drinking heavily and had been deeply in debt when they married. Apparently suffering from a depressive illness, he became convinced his wife was being unfaithful and even contacted a detective agency to enquire about surveillance. After his arrest, he informed the police that his wife had told him she had had several affairs since their marriage.

In fact Jeanette had formed a friendship with 44-year-old Norman Black, a driving instructor. They had met in August and he had lent a sympathetic ear to her marital problems. He asked her out for a drink and their friendship blossomed. When Adam Tadd learnt of it, he wrote a letter threatening to kneecap Black. Because of a misunderstanding, he approached the wrong Mr Black; this was the last straw for Jeanette and she decided to leave Adam and move in with her lover.

She told Tadd their marriage was over but he would not accept it. On the night of the murder, she had returned to her parents' house to collect some of her clothes. Norman Black was supposed to meet her parents there and then drive her to his home. Unfortunately he was delayed and, when he phoned to apologise, was told the devastating news.

Tadd was arrested at his brother's house in Hersham soon after the murder. During his trial at the Old Bailey the following year he pleaded guilty to manslaughter claiming that, at the time of the murder, he had been suffering from diminished responsibility. His plea was accepted by the Crown and he was jailed for five years.

Another twin

Woking signed a charter of friendship in 1993 with Le Plessis-Robinson in France, her second twin town. Links were first established in the previous year. Six kilometres west of Paris, Le Plessis-Robinson is a flourishing town that still boasts a number of peaceful parks and gardens. Its strange name originates from a restaurateur's fascination with the story of *Robinson Crusoe*. In 1848, Joseph Gueusquin, confusing that novel with *Swiss Family Robinson*, decided to build a restaurant in a tree as he thought that Crusoe had made his home in a tree house. He called the surrounding area after his hero and the name Robinson was retained and tree restaurants became popular.

Like Woking, the town is close to the capital and has easy rail and motorway access so attracts businesses. As with Amstelveen, Woking has formed many links and in 1998 a *Place Woking* was erected in the new town centre of Le Plessis-Robinson.

1994

Centenary

This was the year that *The Woking News and Mail* celebrated its centenary. It had first made its appearance as the *Woking News* on 19 October 1894 and for a hundred years it had maintained its high standard and kept to the editorial policy set out in its first edition: 'We will be neither Conservative nor Liberal, but will assume and maintain an attitude of perfect independence.'

A year after the first edition of the *News* appeared, a rival paper, the *Woking Mail*, came into being, promising to be more 'entertaining' than its serious sister paper. When the Woodbridge Press bought both papers, they were merged into *The Woking News and Mail*. In 1964 the paper was bought by the Surrey Advertiser Group which, in 1979, sold 90 per cent of its papers to the *Guardian* and *Manchester Evening News* group.

To celebrate the centenary, the *Woking News and Mail* brought out a souvenir centenary-supplement. The front cover was that of the first edition in 1894 and the whole page was covered in advertisements, apart from a green centenary section in the middle. Inside were fascinating articles covering the history of Woking over the past hundred years. Among many others, there were pieces on famous local residents, shopping 'before the supermarket was king', surrounding villages, recreation and, of course, an article on the newspaper itself. The back cover advertised the more modern Peacocks centre and its attractions.

Gunned down at her front door

In this year there were at least five murders in Woking but the most dramatic was that of Karen Reed on 30 April. There is no doubt that it was a case of mistaken identity and that the intended victim was Karen's sister, Alison Ponting, who worked for the BBC World Service. In 1988 she had married a Russian art dealer and they came to live in England. In March 1993 he was arrested by the British police for two murders apparently ordered by the Russian KGB. He was given two life sentences but the story did not end there. The long arm of the Russian gangsters stretched out to a quiet suburban road on an April evening in 1994 and an innocent woman lay dead in her doorway.

Alison Ponting had been staying with her sister but, on that fatal night, she was not at home when her sister opened her front door to a man apparently delivering a pizza. Karen Reed never received it. There were six gunshots and she fell with bullet wounds in her chest. By the time the ambulance arrived, she was dead and the gunman had disappeared.

Because they had felt Alison Ponting was in danger, the police had also warned her sibling to be on her guard and not open the door to strangers. They had even installed security equipment and panic alarms in her house. But on that fatal day Karen forgot their warnings and she paid for her carelessness with her life. Tight security surrounded the funeral and Alison hid her grief under a thick, black veil. In spite of an exhaustive search, the murderer was never found but the police were convinced it had all the hallmarks of a professional killing.

Crime of passion

Another murder in the same year was definitely a crime of passion. Just before ten o'clock on the morning of Wednesday, 4 May, Julia Wright, brandishing a kitchen knife, walked into her husband's surgery in Old Woking and stabbed his secretary, Fiona Wood, thirty-five times. Then, covered in her victim's blood, she drove to the Nuffield hospital where her husband, gynaecologist Jeremy Wright, was working and told him that she had just killed his mistress.

Julia Davidson had met Jeremy Wright when they were both working at Whipps Cross hospital. They married in June 1979 and Julia gave up her career as a doctor to concentrate on raising their four children. They lived in Hook Heath Avenue in Woking and Jeremy became a respected surgeon. In 1986 Fiona Wood started to work at his surgery as a medical secretary. In 1993 they started an affair. Julia loved her husband and was furious to learn that he had taken a mistress.

After the murder, she was arrested and charged but was eventually found guilty of the lesser charge of manslaughter on the grounds of diminished responsibility. She was given a four-year sentence.

Cards are ace

An important event that occurred in 1994 was the triumph of the local football team, the Woking Cardinals. On Saturday, 20 May, Woking station was awash with red-and-white scarves, peaked caps sporting the Woking badge and general euphoria. The whole of Woking, it seemed, was on its way to Wembley to watch the team play Runcorn in the FA Trophy final.

Ten thousand tickets had been sold and, from all over Surrey, coaches headed towards the famous stadium. In the crowd of nearly 16,000, Woking fans vastly outnumbered those of their opponents. It was an exciting match and when the final whistle blew on a Woking victory, the fans erupted and then disappeared behind an erratically undulating red-and-white curtain of flags.

Euphoria reigned on the route through London and then Waterloo station was invaded by the army of fans wearing red-and-white caps, red-and-white scarves and anything else they could find of the same colour. They enthusiastically waved their flags, whirled rattles and blew on whistles and other available instruments. It was a good-natured crowd, thrilled at the success of the local team.

The following week it was the turn of the town to be festooned with red and white. The team, holding aloft the trophy, paraded through the decorated streets past cheering crowds. Their journey ended at Woking leisure centre where they were honoured at a civic reception. The twentieth of May 1994 is a day that Woking will long remember.

Demolition man

In November a community play called *Running Red* was performed in Woking. It celebrated the writing, a century previously, of *The War of the Worlds* by H. G. Wells. The author wrote his best-known novel while living in Maybury Road, Woking, and it was published in 1898; he left the town soon afterwards. Perhaps he felt guilty because, according to him, the town had been razed to the ground by the deadly invaders from Mars.

The play, *Running Red,* like its predecessor, was set in the future and was fittingly performed in the Wells Suite in the complex known as the Planets – both names reminiscent of the great author. Born in 1866, he died in London on 13 August 1946 but will always have a special place in the hearts of Woking residents, who have long since forgiven him for having demolished their town in his masterpiece.

1995

Flush with cash

When his BMW broke down in the High Street, opera singer Richard Winsborough of Goldsworth Park, rang for a mechanic and then went to buy a new filter. He returned to find a parking ticket on his car. He was not pleased. He was even more annoyed when the council refused to accept his appeal. To illustrate his view of their behaviour, he wrote his cheque on a toilet seat and presented it to Woking's Parking Shop. The bank said it was valid but the council was dubious about accepting it!

Cards come up trumps again

Woking Cardinals beat Kidderminster Harriers by two goals to one at Wembley on Sunday, 14 May. Their second goal was scored two minutes from the end of extra time and, by winning, they retained the FA Trophy, which they had won for the first time in 1994. In the history of the competition only one other club, Scarborough, had won it in consecutive years.

The following Sunday the victorious team paraded around the town in an open-top bus finishing in the town centre. Then in the Peacocks Centre they signed autographs for their many fans. In the evening there was a civic reception hosted by the mayor.

A funeral after fifty years

In February 1941, 21-year-old RAF pilot John Gilders was on a routine patrol over Kent when his Spitfire crashed into a field. He was listed as missing in action and his plane remained buried for over fifty years. Then, in December 1994, archaeologists were exploring the area when they discovered the plane and the pilot's remains. So after fifty years his family was finally able to give him a proper military funeral at Brookwood cemetery in May 1995.

The service was led by Reverend David Osborn, a squadron leader from RAF Uxbridge. The coffin, draped in a Union Jack, was carried by four young RAF officers and was followed by John's younger brother, now seventy, and his two daughters. There was no gun salute but the 'Last Post' was played by a single bugler.

A fitting end

In the Queen's birthday honours' list, Jill Ferguson, principal of Woking sixth-form college, was awarded an OBE for her services to education. It was a fitting end to her career as she retired in July at the end of the school year.

She started teaching in Woking in 1963 and became head of the Girls' Grammar School ten years later. Then in 1977 she was appointed deputy principal of the new college and became principal in 1980. She intended to use her 'retirement' to study for a second degree in modern Italian and Greek. Her first degree had been in Classics.

The Surrey puma

Was it the latest sighting of the Surrey puma? One evening in July a Hook Heath resident was startled to see a tree shaking in his garden. Then he saw a strange animal leap on to the grass and vanish through the hedge. Between three and four feet long, it was black with a long tail and large head.

The grass around the 'shaking' tree had been flattened, there were new scratch marks on the trunk and there was a strange smell in the area. Over the past few weeks, there had been about sixty sightings of the 'puma' in Surrey but it had not yet been properly identified.

1996

Mysterious death

On 29 December 1995, 39-year-old Sharon Hammond was having dinner with her family in Blubeckers restaurant. It was a bitterly cold night and she was wearing a short, black evening-dress. She had had her starter and decided to pay a visit to the ladies' room. It would be the last time she was seen alive.

On 4 January 1996 her body was discovered in a field in Ottershaw four or five miles away from the restaurant. She had died of hypothermia. A motorist later said that he had seen a figure fitting her description walking along the road and he had had to swerve to avoid her. It had been difficult to see her in her black dress. She had been suffering from depression but why she had chosen to walk several miles to her death in the middle of a family dinner party is a mystery.

Mad cow

In the early hours of Saturday morning, 1 June, Woking police received an urgent call to say a mad bull was trotting down the A320 towards Woking. The animal was sighted running towards the Mayford roundabout and into Saunders Lane, stampeding over the village bowling-green. The police chased it along Hook Heath and into Triggs Lane. It had horns and charged the police but it was five hours before they were finally able to capture the fugitive.

It turned out not to be a 'mad bull' after all, but a 2-year-old heifer that had escaped from a field in Sutton Green. The farmer who owned her – Alexander Miller of Bonnishot farm in Worplesdon – said she was so docile that he usually had to push her to get her to move at all.

Green fingers

In August Woking won both the Wyevale Trophy for the South-East in Bloom and the Tidy Britain award. The judges of the latter described Woking's presentation as 'of the highest standard'.

Another close encounter?

One evening during the winter of 1996 the residents of an isolated house on Chobham Common, which was set in 200 acres, looked out of a first-floor window and were puzzled by what they saw. Had there been another murder in the area? Was that a police helicopter hovering in the distance?

They soon realised that what they were seeing was no helicopter. In fact it did not resemble anything they had ever seen. It was the wrong shape for either a plane or a balloon and it was silent. It was a huge, flat, oval shape surrounded with red-and-green lights. Down the centre, white lights flashed as it came closer and looked as though it was about to land on the Common.

Bemused, the watchers stared at the phenomenon for at least ten minutes until it changed direction and disappeared into the distance. They then decided to phone the Meteorological Office. The official was polite but denied knowledge of any flying saucers in the area. It was definitely nothing to do with them.

What was it they saw? The mystery remains.

1997

Sir Alec

Alec Bedser, now seventy-eight, became a knight in the New Year honours' list. He said that he felt 'very honoured'.

Runaway horse

It is not unusual to see horses being ridden on the roads around Woking. Cars give way to them and they are usually well behaved. However, one rider was not so lucky. While trotting demurely down Woodham Road, her horse became restive and threw her off. It then crossed the Six Cross Roads roundabout and headed up the A320.

Fortunately the rider was not hurt. She collected her car and drove around looking for her horse. She couldn't find it but, when she finally returned home, she discovered it had arrived there before her and was behaving as if nothing had happened.

Orlando rocked

In May BBC Television's *Antiques Roadshow* came to the leisure centre and more than 3,500 queued up to have their treasures viewed and valued. The most interesting find was an eighteenth-century German cabinet inlaid with ivory. The furniture expert, Orlando Rock, was thrilled. He described it as 'sensational' and told the bemused owner that it was worth £30,000. Another resident had bought a painting by Robert MacBeth for £550 at an auction. It was now worth more than £10,000.

The team enjoyed their visit and it was certainly a memorable day for Woking.

Golden jubilee

1947 was the year Princess Elizabeth had married her handsome Prince. Fifty years later Queen Elizabeth II and her husband celebrated their golden jubilee. Among other events a garden party was held at Buckingham Palace to which other couples who had been married the same year were invited. Among them were Reg and Ruby Chown from Maybury and Frederick and Joyce Davis from Goldsworth Park. Reg and Ruby had been married at St John's church on 9 July 1947.

'Madonna' parade

In July a statue of the Madonna, which had been venerated in Sicily since 1530, paid a visit to Woking and was paraded through the streets; she was accompanied by a priest from Mussomeli, the statue's home town and followed by hundreds of local Italians and Sicilians. Our Lady of Miracles, as the statue was called, was taken to St Dunstan's church where she remained for a week; she then continued her tour round England before returning home.

Robinson's closes

After trading for sixty years, Robinson's department store finally closed.

Dodi buried at Brookwood

After the horrendous crash in August in Paris in which Princess Diana and Dodi Al Fayed both died, the latter, according to Muslim custom, was buried in the Muslim cemetery at Brookwood within twenty-four hours of his death. In November his remains were exhumed and reburied in their final resting place in the grounds of the Al Fayed family home in Oxted.

Remembering Diana

On 5 September crowds flocked to a memorial service at Christ Church to remember Princess Diana. It was led by the vicar, Malcolm Herbert, and was very moving. The church was packed and many people were standing in the aisles. Afterwards there was a queue to sign the book of condolence and record a message. Many candles were also lit in memory of the Princess.

1998

David Robinson MBE

David Robinson who, with his sister, had run Robinson's department store until its closure in 1997, was awarded an MBE in the New Year honours list. He had lived in Grange Road, Horsell, for many years.

A Martian comes to Woking

The H. G. Wells novel, *The War of the Worlds*, was first published in novel form in 1898 although it had been serialised two years' earlier. To celebrate the centenary, Woking council commissioned artist Michael Condron to put his imagination to work. He created a stainless-steel statue that he called *The Martian Landing*. It was installed in Crown Passage and the manager of a nearby store complained about the disruption caused during its installation.

About seven metres tall, the legs were set wide apart as if it was stalking its prey and the surface had been electroplated to make it shine. The visor on its 'head' shone even more brightly than the rest of it and gave the impression of an all-seeing eye. To make it realistic, it was given a heat ray but, unfortunately, the fumes from the equipment used to fit it to the tripod set-off fire alarms in nearby Crown House.

The 'Martian' was officially unveiled by television presenter Carol Vorderman on the evening of 8 April; the media flocked to Woking and the town was given plenty of coverage in the national newspapers. Miss Vorderman told the crowd that this was the best new work of art she had seen.

The statue was controversial and not everyone liked it. However, the council was interested to receive a phone call from a gentleman in Harrow; he said he was a medium and had been in touch with Wells, who was 'delighted with the statue'. The caller turned down an invitation to attend the unveiling as he was unemployed and couldn't afford the fare!

Widow publishes hero's autobiography

In 1998 a fascinating book was published by a Woking widow. 'Bunnie' Oliver decided to publish the journal of her late husband as a memorial to him. Albert Oliver had been a Battle of Britain pilot and had spent some of the war in prison camps. His story was fascinating. The book was entitled *Kriegie*, the nickname given to prisoners of war by the Italians.

'Ollie' returned to Britain from sunny Trinidad at the outbreak of the second world war in 1939 to enlist in the RAF. He was recruited as a rear gunner – possibly the most dangerous position in the aircraft. He flew a number of missions over Germany before being shot down over Italy. He only just managed to bail out before the plane was engulfed in flames, in which one of the crew died. He was eventually captured and taken to the first Italian prisoner-of-war camp to be built.

From there he was moved to various other camps including the famous Stalag-Luft 111 camp in Poland. The first duty of an RAF officer on being taken prisoner was to try to escape and Ollie took his duties seriously. Unfortunately his earlier attempts were unsuccessful and he was recaptured and placed in solitary confinement.

At Stalag-Luft 111 he was involved in the escape immortalised by Eric Williams in his book, *The Wooden Horse*. When he was invited to join the now-famous escape scheme he commented drily, 'I did not realise I was being recruited as a gymnast' and he notes that he was 'slaving away daily with no hope of sharing the spoils'. His gymnastic activities triggered pain in his back, which he had injured when he landed heavily on the ground because his parachute had failed to open properly. The lack of proper food in the camp also caused an acute attack of food poisoning and he was eventually diagnosed as having stomach ulcers. On the strength of this diagnosis, he was repatriated.

Returning to Trinidad after the war, he met and married a Canadian girl and in 1971 they retired to Woking where he died in 1996.

1999

An historic day

In April, Prince Charles came to Woking and officially opened the Surrey History Centre in Goldsworth Road. As he had studied archaeology and anthropology at Cambridge, he said he was 'delighted' to perform the opening. The site had originally been Goldsworth School and he met some former pupils. Sixty of them had been invited to the opening. They now had a new school in Arthur's Bridge Road.

In the town square the Prince did a walkabout and chatted to many in the crowd. He was impressed with the two double-decker buses that had been funded by the Prince's Trust and were on display. They provided mobile youth-centres for youngsters who lived in isolated communities. The Prince also visited Woking business park in Sheerwater where, at McLaren's, he met Formula One racing champion Mika Hakkinen and saw the winning car.

Coupons and camouflage

In October, the history centre held a fascinating evening called 'Coupons and Camouflage'. Billed as 'an evening of forties' film and food', it provided an opportunity for many Woking residents, who had served on the home front during the war, to relive their experiences. There was an exhibition of letters, ration books, whistles, helmets and other paraphernalia including Vincent Field's 1942 fire-watching book donated to the centre by his widow. A talk about the local Home Guard was followed by a wartime film about civil defence, which had been made for recruitment purposes.

The refreshments served showed that the 'cooks' had done thorough research. Among other forties' culinary delights were spam sandwiches, carrot tarts and eggless cakes. It was an interesting evening organised by a young archivist who had not even been born when the war ended in 1945.

Encore

To celebrate the millennium, the newly formed Rhoda McGaw Theatre Company staged a production containing songs, dances and play extracts from the past one hundred years. They were linked by a narration that also introduced topical events of the time. *Encore* was designed to give the audience the feel of the twentieth century in a short space of time.

It was directed by Maggie Lilley who said it would 'keep the Rhoda alive and kicking over the Christmas and millennium celebrations'. The final script was devised by Lilley, whose idea it had been, Mike Carter, the musical director, Gerry Festa, Jenny Lowde and Richard Parish. It had a cast of thirty actors, singers and dancers with six musicians.

Described as a 'stunning theatrical kaleidoscope', the show opened on 28 December and ran into the next century with the final night on 8 January 2000. The cast was, however, permitted to have free evenings on New Year's Eve and New Year's Day! Every evening, packed audiences of all ages enjoyed the company's celebration of the past century.

The millennium

Like the rest of the world, Woking celebrated the end of the millennium in style. Fairy lights decorated Town Square and crowds gathered beside Christ Church for a service led by the vicar, Malcolm Herbert, assisted by the church band and singers. It was a moving occasion not noticeably dampened by the drizzle of rain. Afterwards the crowds went into the church to partake of hot chocolate. Around the walls were large sheets of paper on which people wrote their hopes and prayers for the future.

At midnight the council provided a spectacular firework display to herald the new century. It was organised from the roof of the car park in Victoria Way and the fireworks could be seen for miles around. Afterwards, passers-by greeted each other and cars hooted in celebration. One group of revellers – members of a rambling club – went on an hour-long walk around the town ending at the former home of playwright George Bernard Shaw in Maybury before returning home.

2000

They also serve

On 3 March the Queen unveiled the home-front memorial at a service in Coventry Cathedral. It was to commemorate all those who had served on the home front during the second world war and done so much to help the war effort. Two days' later, on Sunday, 5 March, a similar service was held at Guildford Cathedral. As Woking is in the diocese of Guildford, many Woking residents were invited to attend. Some of them had actually served on the home front while others were the sons and daughters of those who had. There were also a number of ex-servicemen present.

It was a moving service attended by many local dignitaries including the chairman of Surrey County Council, the High Sheriff of Surrey and the Lord Lieutenant of Surrey. In his introduction, the sub dean paid tribute to all who had served on the home front who 'were not formally recognised and thanked by the nation at the time'. He told the congregation, 'We owe it to them to put that omission right.'

During the service there were reminiscences from representatives of the Land Army, the Bevin Boys and the Air Transport Auxiliary. The latter was a tiny, uniformed, bemedalled lady who had actually flown planes to France. Following the short talks, a moving rendition of 'Amazing Grace' was played by a young Scottish piper on the bagpipes. The sermon was given by Canon Eric James who had formerly been the Queen's chaplain. The service ended with the singing of all three verses of the national anthem.

Marie Carlile Home closes

In December, to the great regret of many Woking residents, Marie Carlile Home closed. It had been a Church Army residential home since the 1950s and had always provided an excellent standard of care for its elderly residents. Wilson Carlile had founded the Church Army in 1882 and during his latter years had lived in the house with his sister, Marie Carlile, after whom the building was named.

There was great consternation about the decision and many irate letters were written to Church Army headquarters. The home had served the community well for nearly half a century and it was with great sadness that relatives and friends of the residents, local clergy and many others packed into the small chapel for a farewell service led by the vicar of Christ Church, Malcolm Herbert. Tributes were paid to Church Army captain, Jim Etheridge, and his wife, Margaret, who had run the home for many years.

2001

Never too late

On 2 February Violet Marie married the man of her dreams at Weybridge register office. She had first met Stafford Hamilton in August 2000 at the Vyne day centre in Knaphill where they were both attending a party to celebrate the Queen Mother's one-hundredth birthday.

Stafford said that it had been love at first sight and proposed four months later. After the wedding they had a four-day honeymoon in Sidmouth in Devon. They both lived in Goldsworth Park and the unusual aspect of their love story was that they were both in their seventies.

Visit to Number 10

Woking's MP, Humphrey Malins, was one of those selected to take a group of children from his constituency to visit 10 Downing Street and have tea with the prime minister and his wife. The lucky pupils were Sadia Ali from New Monument school, Krystal-Lee Drameh from Woking High School and Ronak Darafshian from Bishop David Brown School. They were taken on a tour of the Houses of Parliament before being shown round one of the most famous residences in the world. Their visit to London ended with afternoon tea with Tony and Cherie Blair.

Sir Alec remembers

On 25 February Sir Donald Bradman, one of the greatest batsmen the world has ever known, died at the age of ninety-two in Adelaide, Australia. Sir Alec Bedser, who, with his twin, Eric, lived in Carlton Road, reminisced about the great man with whom he had been friends for over fifty years. When Alec

Bedser dismissed him for a duck, Bradman commented that it had been 'the best ball I faced in my whole career'.

A third twin

Links between Rastatt in Germany and Woking were first forged in 1999 and the final signing took place at the Grand Baroque Palace in Rastatt in April. Three hundred guests watched the mayor of Rastatt, Herr Klaus-Eckhard, and Woking's mayor, Ian Eastwood, sign the charter of friendship. Afterwards a string quartet entertained the audience with music by Mozart and Purcell.

Situated in south-west Germany, Rastatt is bordered by the Rhine and the Black Forest. It not only contains a number of eighteenth-century buildings but also boasts a meadowlands area where rare wildlife is legally protected. Like Woking, the town has excellent transport facilities and is a popular business location.

Woking mourns

On Tuesday, 11 September two planes crashed into New York's World Trade Centre and the world was plunged into mourning. Woking's mayor, Barry Pope, led tributes to the victims and the borough council sent a letter of condolence on behalf of local people to the American embassy in London. A book of condolence was opened in the reception area of the civic offices and crowds queued to sign it.

On Friday Woking stopped for a three-minute silence to remember the dead and a special ceremony was held at the Mosque to pray for those affected by the tragedy. The Imam, Pir Qadri, said, 'Islam condemns the people who did this brutal act.' Those affected were also remembered in prayer at all the Woking churches on Sunday morning.

The following Tuesday at one o'clock a special memorial service was held at Christ Church; members of the council, community leaders, the Imam and many members of the public attended. The church was packed. The vicar, Malcolm Herbert, conducted the service and the Bishop of Guildford, John Gladwin, gave the address.

At least two Woking residents were in New York at the time of the disaster but were not injured. Charlotte Fiddler, the daughter of a former mayor of Woking, was involved in a fashion shoot in Times Square – barely a quarter of a mile away – when the first plane crashed into the twin towers. Tim Pearce, son of a former editor of the *Woking News and Mail*, was actually heading for the World Trade Centre when he heard the explosion. Neither Charlotte nor Tim was able to contact their families until much later.

A fireman from Virginia Water, who was working in New York, was one of those who died. In December three firemen from Woking went to New York to show support for their colleagues there. They visited Ground Zero where the twin towers had stood, and one of them remarked, 'The emptiness hits you.' They attended a memorial service in the Bronx and signed books of condolence.

2002

Lost in Woking

Richard Meredith – an intrepid traveller, who had backpacked round the world – wrote a book about his experiences entitled *One Way or Another*. It was on sale at Ottakar's bookshop in Woking and he had been invited to attend a signing session to launch it. Unfortunately, he arrived half an hour late. Although he had travelled round the world, he found it almost impossible to negotiate Woking's complicated road system!

When he eventually managed to discover the multi-storey car park, he found that he had insufficient change to pay for a ticket. Luckily, a local motorist took pity on him and was able to provide him with the necessary coins and the signing session, although late in starting, proved very successful.

Schoolboy hero

In June Hayley Powell, who lived in Horsell, panicked when her electric cooker suddenly burst into flames. Her two young children were both asleep in the bedroom. Rushing out of the smoke-filled kitchen, she ran next door. Fourteen-year-old Khaleeq Khan, a pupil at Horsell High School, came to her rescue. Although suffering from asthma, he ran to her house, coughed his way through the kitchen and up the stairs to the children's bedroom.

Dragging 4-year-old Reanne from her bed, he carried her downstairs and out into the fresh air. When Hayley screamed that 2-year-old Owain was still in the house, Khaleeq went back though the dense smoke to search for the toddler. Choking with the fumes, he eventually located him huddled underneath the duvet and carried him out to join his relieved mother.

In December, at Westminster Abbey, Khaleeq was one of eleven children to receive the *Woman's Own* Children of Courage award for his bravery.

Grand opening

Friday 14 June was an important day for Knaphill; it was the grand opening of Knaphill lower school. For many years, there had been setbacks in the proposals to build a much-needed new school.

In 1945 temporary classrooms were erected on the site to house secondary school pupils as the school-leaving age had been raised. In 1968 the 'temporary' buildings were taken over by the infant school. 1975 saw the erection of a nursery unit and twenty years later a terrapin unit was put up. With the original buildings, the temporary buildings and the extras, the site now consisted of seven separate buildings – not an ideal situation for young children. In spite of this, Beacon status was awarded to the school in 1999 because of its achievements.

Work on the new school finally started in July 2000. The staff continued to teach their pupils while demolition and rebuilding went on all around them. There was yet another delay when underground concrete bunkers, used during the second world war, were discovered under the site.

At last the new building was completed and declared officially open by the vice-chairman of Surrey County Council, Mrs Sheila Gruselle. The afternoon was a pleasant occasion as the children sang to an invited audience who later toured the impressive new school before partaking of refreshments.

Judo success

In September at the Commonwealth Games in Manchester, judo enthusiast, Sam Lowe, from Goldsworth Park, won a gold medal. Then, in December, she was also the joint winner in the student category of the *Sunday Times* sportswoman of the year awards.

Rapist caught

During the year women from Woking were terrified to go out after dark or to walk alone in wooded areas. A serial rapist was prowling around the south-east of England and two girls had been attacked in the Woking area. In July an 18-year-old was raped in Goldsworth Park and six weeks' later, in a wood near Pyrford Common Road, a 13-year-old suffered the same fate.

In December, Antoni Adam Imiela from Kent was arrested and charged with nine rapes including the two in Woking. Women in the area could now feel safer knowing the rapist was in police custody.

2003

Murder!

Ireneu and Paula Injai married in 1999 and had a son. However, the marriage did not last long and in August 2002 they separated; Paula remained in their house in Camberley while Ireneu went to live in Maybury Road, Woking.

Injai saw his son frequently but as a court order forbade him to go within 500 yards of his wife's house, he always collected the boy from a nearby petrol station. Paula, meanwhile, found herself a new partner and her husband was furious. He could not bear the thought of his son being brought up by another man. He telephoned the new boyfriend and demanded to know if he had been sleeping with his wife.

On 8 January 2003 Paula made the biggest mistake of her life. She took her young son to her ex-husband's house and confirmed that there *was* a new man in her life. He lost control and attacked her, stabbing her in the neck so savagely that the blade snapped. He also bit her neck and shoulder and then ripped the rings from her fingers.

Then he took his 2-year-old son and left the flat. He went to a friend's house and said he had taken his wife's rings so that he could sell them to help pay debts. Neighbours had called the police when they heard screaming from the flat but, by the time they arrived, Injai had disappeared. They found Paula's body on a bed covered by a bloodstained duvet.

Injai was later arrested and charged with murder. He was sent for trial at the Old Bailey in September. He pleaded not guilty to murder but guilty of manslaughter because he said his wife had attacked him first. The jury did not believe him and found him guilty of murder. The judge sentenced him to life imprisonment for the 'horrendous crime'.

Attacked by a peacock

It was one of those lovely warm days in July when Lisa and Stuart Stuart-Runsey of Brookwood decided to take their new Ford car for a drive. It was a midnight-blue Ford KA; they had only bought it in April and were very proud of it.

They decided to visit the Burpham Court farm park where they could wander round and feed the animals. They parked the car in the designated parking space and wandered off. They bought some pellets to feed the sheep, gazed at the llamas and admired the peacocks which, although they had lost some of their tail feathers, still strutted as if they were the proud owners of the farm.

When the couple returned to their car at the end of a pleasant afternoon, they were horrified. A large peacock was sitting on it, admiring himself in the reflection in the blue paintwork. He was not only sitting; his claws were busily occupied in scratching a decoration on the pristine blue paint and lumps had been gouged out of the bumper. Stuart rushed towards the creature and tried to hustle it away but it gave him a disdainful stare and continued with its handiwork.

Then it discovered the wing mirrors. They, of course, were even better for catering to its vanity; there was no way it was going to be prised away from admiring itself in a *real* mirror. Stuart and Lisa were desperate. Their car would need a lot of pampering before it returned to its pre-peacock state. The farmer, hastily summoned, showed little sympathy and pointed out that the car had been parked at their own risk.

The insurance company was more sympathetic but could offer no help. The car wasn't insured against being attacked by a peacock! Sadly, the couple went to the garage and explained what had happened. After he had finished laughing, the mechanic said he'd had to deal with other cars with the same problem. However, peacocks only attacked blue and green cars, he informed them. No doubt those colours will be avoided when the couple buy their next car!

Fuel cell

In June, Woking acquired the distinction of being the first borough in the country to be powered by a fuel cell. Hydrogen and oxygen would be fed into the cell to produce electricity and water. The idea originated from Sir William Grove who developed it at the London Institute during the 1840s while he was professor of physics.

The Woking fuel cell was situated in a newly landscaped garden in Woking Park, which would be irrigated by water from it. The garden was named Grove Garden in honour of Sir William and a statue of the physicist stood nearby. A surrounding mural by Alan Potter detailed the history of the cell. The mayor of Woking, Richard Sanderson, performed the opening of the fuel cell and unveiled the statue in front of a number of distinguished guests including descendants of Sir William.

2004

The Gordon memorial service

On Sunday, 25 January the Gordon memorial service of Gordon's School was held at Guildford Cathedral. The service is held annually on the date nearest both to General Gordon's birthday and the date of his murder. Until 1963 it was held either in London or the provinces. Both St Paul's Cathedral and Westminster Abbey had hosted the service. In 1963 it was held for the first time at Guildford Cathedral and has been held there ever since.

The Cathedral was packed with proud parents and pupils wearing their distinctive tartan uniforms. The sixth formers, looking very smart in black suits, acted as ushers. It was a moving service with the pipe lament, 'Flowers of the Forest', played on the bagpipes by Troy Houghton, in honour of Gordon. The congregation sang the rousing hymns, including 'Jerusalem', with enthusiasm and the sermon was given by David Cooper, senior chaplain at Eton College.

Rapist jailed

In January the trial of Antoni Imiela – the serial rapist who had attacked two Woking girls – started at Maidstone Crown Court. The attacks had taken place between November 2001 and October 2002. Imiela was finally arrested on 2 December 2002. During the enquiry, police officers from six different forces worked closely together and DNA-tested over 3,500 men. It was the sample taken from Imiela that convinced police that they had found their man.

After a trial lasting nearly three months, the jury of seven men and five women found Imiela guilty of most of the charges including the rape of the 13-year-old girl on Pyrford Common in September 2002. Mr Justice Owen ordered the two charges relating to the attacks on the 18-year-old in Goldsworth Park to remain on the court file as the jury could not reach a verdict. He described Imiela as 'a ruthless sexual predator' and sentenced him to seven life sentences, so it was unlikely he would ever again be able to stalk the streets in search of victims.

BIBLIOGRAPHY

W. H. Johnson, *Surrey Murder Casebook* (Countryside Books, 2000)

A. E. V. Oliver, *Kriegie* (George Mann Books, 1998)

Memories of Woking (True North Books Limited, 2000)

J. R. and S. E. Whiteman, *Victorian Woking* (Surrey Archaeological Society)

Methold engineering Ltd: 50 years of service (Written by the family)

Iain Wakeford, *Changing Woking 1900–1929* (Woking Community Play Association)

Peter Wichman, *Christ Church, Woking: A Centenary History* (Send and Ripley Historical Society, 1991)

The Spirit of Brooklands (souvenir booklet)

Sheerwater Pylon: The First 10 Years (Compiled by Iain Wakeford for the Sheerwater Neighbourhood Watch, 2002)

Lieutenant Colonel Derek Bond, Royal Engineers, *The Gordon Heritage* (Robert Hale, 1985)

Alan Crosby, *A History of Woking* (Phillimore & Co, Ltd, 2003)

Iain Wakeford, *Bygone Woking*: (Phillimore & Co. Ltd, 1993)

Heritage leaflets produced by Iain Wakeford

Leaflets produced by Woking Borough Council

Leaflets and newsletters produced by the Woking Town Twinning Association